MADAM
MOHINI

MADAM MOHINI

A ROMANTIC TALE OF VIOLENCE

KAMAL GILL

www.whitefalconpublishing.com

Madam Mohini
A Romantic Tale of Violence
Kamal Gill

www.whitefalconpublishing.com

All rights reserved
First Edition, 2022
© Kamal Gill, 2022
Cover design by White Falcon Publishing, 2022
Cover image by Kamal Gill

No part of this publication may be reproduced, or stored in a retrieval system, or transmitted in any form by means of electronic, mechanical, photocopying or otherwise, without prior written permission from the author.

The contents of this book have been certified and timestamped on the POA Network blockchain as a permanent proof of existence. Scan the QR code or visit the URL given on the back cover to verify the blockchain certification for this book.

The views expressed in this work are solely those of the author and do not reflect the views of the publisher, and the publisher hereby disclaims any responsibility for them.

Requests for permission should be addressed to
Kml_gill@yahoo.ca

ISBN - 978-1-63640-638-1

Chapter 1

She stood glancing at the fading light out of the window of her office. There was an uneasy silence in the room. Two pot-bellied men were looking at her, waiting impatiently. Both of them were balding middle-aged men with fat stuffed up to their throats. One of them was wheezing. His belly was pushed up by his thighs and his lungs got squeezed between his throat and stomach as he sat on the sofa. His dark face carried an expression of disgraceful flattering. The other looked like a ruminating buffalo, quite motionless and expressionless. Then he moved. He tilted to the left and his right bottom went up slightly. While he straightened his right leg, his knee cracked grimly. He forced his hand into the right pocket of his trousers and took out a handkerchief and mopped his forehead.

Sukhbir sat in front of them and everyone looked curious.

She held a file. She brought her eyes back to the file and flipped through it casually. The fat men stirred

MADAM MOIIINI - A Romantic Tale of Violence

and exchanged glances. Sukhbir blinked at them. She resumed looking outside. Everyone looked curious again.

A solitary eagle floated in the dim evening sky, lazily dipping and rising with the breeze. The trees stood straighter and taller, puffing out their chests with arrogance. She turned and sat in the chair.

A big photo of the Chief Minister cum Party President hung on the wall behind her. The photo seemed as if he was overlooking and studying the entire ambience with his deep intricate eyes. Already uncertain about the need to go ahead with the deal, she shut the file with a snap and coldly called an end to the meeting.

'But Madam,' one of them stammered in bewilderment.

Sukhbir straightened his shoulders and said politely, 'Madam, they are insisting.'

She frowned slightly and sat up abruptly. Clearing her throat, she came to the point, and said firmly, 'Look, Mr Gupta, this is not a grocery shop'.

Sukhbir's eyes flicked from Madam to the fat men, 'Mr Gupta,' he started with an emphasis, 'you are going to get a Rs 500 crore deal with the grace of Madam. If you find the deal unprofitable, we can give the other party a chance. They will indeed be eager to grab it at any cost'.

The fat men looked helpless. One of them opened his mouth to say something, but after reconsidering, he said nothing. The other man elbowed him. The first

MADAM MOHINI - A Romantic Tale of Violence

man nodded and slowly sighed, 'Right Madam'. He sat up with immense effort and handed over a briefcase to Sukhbir. He bent a little and folded his hands in salutation. The other man followed suit. 'Madam, many, many thanks. Please continue giving us chances to serve you.' His voice was unusually honeyed.

She nodded and grinned. A beam of satisfaction flashed across the fat cheeks of the men as they left the room.

Sukhbir busied himself with some papers. Under the cover of meticulously choosing a piece of paper, he studied Madam. She showed signs of deep contemplation.

Suddenly, she caught his eye on her. 'What?' she asked.

'Nothing,' Sukhbir replied curtly.

'Then why are you looking at me like this?' she queried.

'Madam,' Sukhbir stammered, 'I was only wondering...'

'Yes,' her voice was resolute.

For nearly a minute there was silence between the two. Sukhbir broke the silence and continued, 'Do you mean that... that... are you really quitting?"

'I know,' she spoke slowly. 'It will sound absurd to everyone but all this has lost its purpose to me.'

'But...', Sukhbir wanted to add something.

'All the *buts* in the world won't change anything for me. This final deal that we have just made is enough to sustain me through the rest of my life.'

MADAM MOHINI - A Romantic Tale of Violence

Her words knifed through him. He sat transfixed staring with horror-struck eyes. Her decision sounded a death knell to Sukhbir's career too or so it seemed at that moment.

'Then...' Sukhbir paused, seeming at a loss of words for a moment. But as he opened his mouth again to resume talking, Madam stood up abruptly. 'We will talk later, Sukhbir,' she said very gently.

Sukhbir nodded blankly.

* * * * * * *

Madam sat in the veranda of her bungalow entrenched deep in thoughts and gazed meditatively around her. Her thoughts were none too pleasant, for there was much that was troubling her. She had felt brittle, stiff, and cold throughout the day, trying hard to cover it with an expressionless face, though she looked bleary-eyed and disoriented. She had become disconcertingly silent, her face filled with sadness. Her eyes were fixed on something far beyond which no one else could see. A shadow fell across the whole house. Servants wondered at her indolence and stared at each other. The silence was not abnormal for her. She never spoke much. But today her silence was hard coated with a feeling of helplessness.

The wind picked up and whistled through the trees. The sky was grey. Mist drifted through the garden. A mass of clouds threatened rain. She sat still for a

MADAM MOHINI - A Romantic Tale of Violence

moment. With an effort, she pulled herself together. The noises from the kitchen had started to die down. A utensil clinked reluctantly. Thunder boomed and a few drops of rain began to fall. She went out in the garden. The drops splattered on the earth, filling the air with a moist fragrance. She murmured something to herself, while the rain pattered down on her. She opened her eyes squinting against the rain. It grew heavier plastering her hair to her skull. The house stood silently behind her.

'Madam!' The call didn't register. 'Madam, you will fall ill. It's cold. Please come inside,' said the maid who stood bent and humble behind her. Madam took an unsteady step back and then turned. The maid rushed to open the door and watched as she clambered up the stairs. The faint clatter of her footsteps swam on the silence of the house like scum floating in a pond.

She stood before the mirror in her bedroom, combing out the damp hair. It had been incredibly long since she had visited her house in the village. The house was a repository of so many memories, painful as well as pleasant. She stared at her reflection in the mirror. She touched a finger to the hair at her temples. When had they turned grey? Suddenly, she felt weary. In bed, gazing absently at the ceiling, some syllables of grief erupted from her lips. She pressed her forehead against the pillow and squeezed her eyes shut.

* * * * * * *

That night also, she could barely sleep. The past filled her mind to the brim. A medley of images, some sharp and bright like a sunny day, but some stood out disconnectedly, like pictures with blackness all around them. She felt a terrible pain. She didn't know whether her decision would save her from this haunting pain or not. As dawn broke, a yellow ray from the rising sun fell through the window. The dark shapes started detaching themselves from the darkness. Their colours slowly emerged in the room. She made an effort to move out of bed, gathered up her hair, and fastened them into a bun. She looked out of the window. The sky was deep blue, flawless, and clear. The sun was unusually bright. An unbearable emptiness filled the air.

11:00 am

She went into her camp office. The house was silent. A thin grey light was seeping through the rooms. Sukhbir waited there. For long he kept speaking without conjuring much response from her. He frequently resettled his specks and paced up and down the room. He made some jerky movements with his hands. But when he spoke his voice was gentle and patient. He was explaining and persuading, at the same time.

She gave a small, non-committal shrug.

At last, he sank into the sofa, frowning into space. What on earth could he do? Why was his voice falling

MADAM MOHINI - A Romantic Tale of Violence

on deaf ears? She was as expressionless as ever. There had always been a layer of hardened shell around her which she relentlessly defended. Neither a twitch on her face nor a quiver on her lips ever defied her defence. Her eyes were inscrutable like dark caverns. Sukhbir too endeavoured to keep this shell as impenetrable as possible for he was very comfortable in this situation. There was no one who could be identified as a relative or a friend of hers. She stood as alone and magnificent as a solitary tree on a hilltop. For the last eight years, since she had become a Minister, Sukhbir had been managing all matters concerning her and all of them were only professional, never personal. Other than Madam, there wasn't anyone to be pleased and a complete interference-free atmosphere prevailed. There were frequent gossips about her, but she herself never spoke about any of her acquaintances. If someone approached him with a request for an appointment with Madam with an allusion to some old connection, he would at once reject the request on one pretext or the other.

His feet made a convulsive movement. He had not stirred from his seat, but his mind was running swiftly. He desperately needed to break the ice between them.

'You can tell me if you want,' numbness stole over Sukhbir as he spoke, watching her closely. Madam's mind seemed highly exercised. She gazed around with faded eyes. The silk curtains at the windows waved in the light breeze.

MADAM MOHINI - A Romantic Tale of Violence

'Well, it's of no great consequence anymore.' She leaned back in her chair with her eyes closed and her head sunk into the backrest. She half-opened her lids and glanced across at Sukhbir.

'You have grown old gracefully, Madam,' Sukhbir smiled tremulously.

'Yes, time has passed... The seasons when mangoes ripen on trees have come and gone with one spring season following another. Roses bloomed and withered away but thorns stayed,' she reminisced softly.

Sukhbir moved to a chair across the table. His breath quivered as the sorrow in Madam's voice filled the room.

'What has happened? You can repose in me, Madam,' Sukhbir uttered, his voice, fainter than a whisper.

Madam inhaled deeply. 'It is not easy for me to tell you the whole story. Every event of my life is seared into my memory.'

'Tell me as much as you can, Madam,' Sukhbir's voice was laden with concern. She seemed to be mining deep in her memory.

'I was a little girl... just eight years...maybe. The year must be 1983.' Her eyes were focused on something far.

'I was playing with my doll, sitting on the *Diwan* lying against a wall in the drawing-room. I spent most of my day on this *Diwan,* doing my homework, playing with my mother-made cloth-dolls, eating lunch and dinner, and finally sleeping at night. The *Diwan* was so placed that my mother and I could observe each other while she

✦ 8 ✦

MADAM MOHINI - A Romantic Tale of Violence

was working in the kitchen. That day she had finished making a new doll for me which had shiny black eyes made out of the buttons from my father's worn-out shirt. She had stuffed its head with cotton and made a pretty frock for her out of a piece of a red silk handkerchief. It was the most beautiful thing I had ever seen.

'Ah! So pretty,' I exclaimed, my excitement was uncontrollable. My mother was happy to see me happy.

But to my bad luck, my stupid mouth uttered unmindfully.

'Mommy, this is my little sister,' and I kissed the doll.

My mother got enraged and shook me by my shoulders.

'Must your black tongue wag... Can't you speak auspicious words?'

My first reaction was bafflement; next, I felt hurt and my eyes welled up at her rebuke. Thirdly, I thought about my uncanny potential for premonitions. But I never hated her for that because I knew that she loved me. Her reaction was a product of her own fear. She was afraid of siring another girl child because of the tremendous social pressure on her. And society is created within a home, it takes a round of the neighbouring streets, pays a visit to some relative, and ends back in the home itself.

My mom was a quiet woman, always lost in her thoughts. She kept doing her household chores impassively. She never stepped out of her home except to buy some things from the street vendors. She never laughed, but she never failed to smile at me when our eyes met. I only heard her laughter on two of the many occasions when a man visited our house. At that time, I didn't know who that man was, but he was definitely handsome and he entered and exited our house secretly; that too when my father was not at home. I knew that my father and mother hated each other but they had to stay together simply because they were married.

The only thing I knew about that man was that his name was Akashdeep Singh and he hailed from the same village called Rumi, where my mother lived with her parents before her marriage.

It was almost eight at night. The *phat-phat* noise of my father's Mitsubishi canter gradually became louder and finally stopped in front of our house, a two-room house in the suburbs of Patiala. A day before when he had come home, he had brought a heavy gunny sack in his canter which he dragged in as fast as he could. My mother opened the door as glumly as ever. He dragged the sack to the storeroom and slid it under a small wooden casket in which my mother kept the two quilts, a blanket, a shawl, and four sweaters at the end of every winter. These were all the objects that guarded the family against the winter chill. On this day, the first thing he did on coming home was to check if the sack was still there. After doing so, he went to the kitchen.

My mother pushed a steel plate towards him with four chapattis, a bowl of chicken curry and mango

MADAM MOHINI - A Romantic Tale of Violence

pickle. He took the plate, sat on one of the low stringed stools and started eating. Over the past few months, chicken — hitherto a luxury — had become a regular part of our meals. My father's earning seemed to have shot up suddenly. My mother filled a steel tumbler with water and sat in front of him on another low stool; her knees close to her chest.

'Got late today?' she asked plainly.

'Hmm,' he replied while chewing a piece of chicken flesh.

My mother looked on waiting for details.

'Today it was my turn to oblige those bastards,' he said after swallowing and then took another morsel.

'CRPF?'

'Hmm... And I did well,' he chuckled and looked at my mother for a brief second. He finished eating, rubbed his fingers on the chequered cloth hanging on his shoulder, and then drank some water.

My mother picked up the plate and threw the bones in the dustbin under the kitchen sink. 'What happened?' She asked without looking away from her work.

'I loosened the bolts of the side supports of my canter. Almost twenty CRPF men were there. I was taking them from Patiala to Rajpura and can you imagine what happened?' he laughed zestfully.

My mother looked at him and shook her head in negation. She was heating milk for him in a saucepan.

MADAM MOHINI - A Romantic Tale of Violence

'Many of them were leaning against the sides of the canter and the sides opened...,' he could not help laughing aloud and continued, 'they tumbled out onto the road like pumpkins. They were lucky that no vehicle was crossing by, otherwise...'

My mother gave a feeble smile, feigning amusement. 'What was the need?' she muttered.

'This is how these mother fuckers will stop calling me for *begar.*' He sounded aggressive. Mother gave him a big brass tumbler brimmed with milk.

'Why haven't you put *kesar* in it?' he asked. 'These good days have come after ages of hardship. Stop being a miser,' he said harshly.

My mother pursed her lips as if trying not to retort and looked away.

'I am talking to you, Bitch!' he got louder.

'Shut up! The little amount of money that you have stashed away has gone to your head. I have to save some for the girl too.' Her voice was low but firm. I tried to concentrate on my doll, pretending ignorance to what was happening between my parents.

'Girl! This useless chunk of flesh that you could produce in seven years of marriage. I want a son.' He held her arm and shook her. 'Did you hear? I want a son,' he screamed. His fingers were digging into her flesh. She winced with pain and tried to wrestle free.

'That is not in my control, you blunt head,' she muttered out of her gnawed teeth.

MADAM MOHINI - A Romantic Tale of Violence

'Oh, is it?' he leaned his neck forward. 'I know for what you are saving the money?' He tightened his grip, 'To serve almonds and milk to your boyfriend.'

I kept my doll aside and pressed my hands over my ears. Such fights were a regular affair in our house.

At that age, I didn't understand much of what was going on around me. Perhaps, my mother was aware of the dangers of the activities that she and my father were involved in — he, in the 'loaded-gunny-sack' business and she with Akashdeep. Though their pursuits were different but both activities were equally dangerous. Therefore, she used to keep instructing me, 'If I make you hide somewhere; make sure you stay there till the time I give you a call.' She would wag her finger pointedly and say, 'In case you hear a din outside, keep on hiding till everything becomes peaceful.' She used to even make me do hiding drills. All this kept me in a state of constant fear at home. The air seemed to be haunted by ghosts and the ground beneath an abode of venomous snakes!

Things were not good at school as well. Many things had changed." Her voice was tinged with zest now. "I remember," she smiled faintly as she became comfortably reminiscent. "You know what was the worst?" Madam asked lightly.

"No," Sukhbir shook his head.

"The uniform..." Both of them let out a low suppressed laughter.

◆ 13 ◆

MADAM MOHINI - A Romantic Tale of Violence

"All the girls as little as five years to as old as fifteen years were made to wear white salwar kameez," Madam said while regaining her poise, "and saffron dupatta," she added. "The kameez was fine but I hated wearing the salwar." She frowned. "Initially, you know my feet got entangled in it and I had some nasty tumbles which hurt and bruised me many times. Going to the washroom was such a big problem, too. It was hard to tie back the salwar on the waist again. At times the pressure was too much and I didn't get a chance to even lower my salwar and it got wet."

Madam's lips slowly parted into a big smile, like an unfolding tulip flower. "Embarrassing though it was, the worst was yet to come. One fine morning when our teacher made me stand up to recite a poem, I was so happy that there was a twinkle in my eyes." Madam narrowed her eyes as if trying hard to recollect. "Hardly had I finished reciting the first sentence when the whole class burst out into hoots of laughter. I looked at them in bewilderment and then I looked at my teacher. She was laughing too. Nothing could be more disastrous. Her grinning teeth were getting dug into my flesh and I could see my blood in her mouth. Then she got up from her chair and came to kneel in front of me. She was still trying hard to control her grin. It was then that I realized that my salwar was at my feet. She pulled it up and tightly tied the knot of the *nada*. After that incident, my mother sympathetically replaced all the

MADAM MOHINI - A Romantic Tale of Violence

nadas in my salwars with elastics. But thereafter, I hated going to school.

In school, many changes were also made in the conduct of the morning assembly. All of us, including our teachers, were made to cover our heads when hymns from the *Guru Granth Sahib* were recited in the morning assembly. And strangely, the singing of the national anthem was stopped. I didn't know what they recited and what it meant. But I was sure that they were praying to God, who my mother had told me was omnipotent, omnipresent, omniscient, and deserved many more 'omni-ous' adjectives. After all, God can't have any religion, this is what I thought at that time. But I was a little kid — immature and naïve. It took me many years to learn the truth about God and by God's mercy, today I know that there are many Gods and ours is the best." She gave a sarcastic smile. "I prayed with concentration and strong emotions because my mother told me that that was how god's favours could be invoked. Moreover, I was told that since a child's heart is pure, its prayers never go unanswered.

In my mother's opinion, all those changes were for good and she encouraged me to adapt to them happily. I knew her opinions were actually Akashdeep's opinions. She often talked with great reverence about a saint. His name was so difficult that for a child of my age it was difficult to even remember it. But as the measure of my spent life increased, the name was heard too frequently

MADAM MOHINI - A Romantic Tale of Violence

to be ignored. He was Jarnail Singh Bhindranwale. My mother considered him a saint and felt that this saint had not only revived the values of the Sikh religion but had kept it away from the evil called 'modernity'. He made Sikhs return to the simple ways of their warrior forefathers and maintain a unique identity. The Saree was declared a Hindu outfit and *bindi* a Hindu fashion. So Sikh women were forbidden from using either of them. My mother told me that his message was being hailed by the masses and people were taking oaths to follow the path shown by him. They baptized themselves and gave up any kind of self-indulgence. As a result, they could work longer hours and raise a better crop.

My mother went on for hours and hours extolling the virtues of this saint. I listened to her with my eyes full of surprise and awe. Everything sounded so utopian.

As I told you, I hated going to school. But my ambitious mother kept pushing me to go to school. Her aim was to see me becoming a doctor. Her aim filled me with dread. I was in the third standard. The mornings when I could perfectly feign a stomach ache, I was allowed to stay home. One such morning, just after my father left, a jeep stopped behind our house. It was Akashdeep. He kissed my cheek.

'How is our *beti* sahib?' he said and patted my head affectionately.

'Fine,' I replied beaming.

MADAM MOHINI - A Romantic Tale of Violence

This was his characteristic way of addressing me. As he would say this, I felt elevated to the status of a princess. He always smiled fondly at me and I could feel the affection gently flowing out of him. I smiled inwardly whenever I thought of him.

He rushed into the bedroom looking for my mother and closed the door behind him. I placed my ear on the door to listen. Even though they were speaking in hushed tones, their voices were audible to me in the silence of the house.

'I am going to Jagraon tonight to execute an important plan,' he was telling my mother and he sounded like a highway robber.

'When will you be back here?' mother sounded worried.

'Hopefully tomorrow,' he replied reassuringly.

'It is not safe for you to stay there for long,' my mother said with concern.

'Don't worry. I attended my sister's wedding also. What could these mother fuckers do?' he said confidently.

'I still curse that day you got into all this,' mother rebuked him.

'You know it was not a choice,' he said imploringly.

'Yes, I know,' she sighed, 'we would have gotten married!'

'You didn't wait for me,' he complained tenderly.

MADAM MOHINI - A Romantic Tale of Violence

'Not me... I was helpless. You know it. How else could I bring your child into this world?' she said softly.

'Leave it... Let bygones be bygones. We have a mission now and the saint is our lighthouse. This is a noble mission. Perhaps, the Guru chose us. We have to free Punjab from these Brahmans.'

'I am with you,' mother told him emphatically.

'This is two lakh rupees. Give it to your husband,' he told her.

'Two guns and five hundred bullets?' Mother confirmed.

'Take care of our daughter,' he told her tenderly.

'Hmmm...' My mother seemed to be in tears.

That day it dawned on me that I had two fathers, one biological and the other, social. When he left, he took the gunny sack along with him. That was the first time I came to know what the gunny sack business was about. As soon as Akashdeep left, my mother sat down on the *Diwan*, with a *gutka* (a handbook of hymns from the Guru Granth Sahib) and covered her head. I saw her lips moving over the prayers which continued for at least an hour. My mother, a poor faithful creature kept praying, but Akashdeep didn't return the next day.

After four days, one gloomy night as all other nights, I was sitting on my mother's lap. My head was resting on her breasts. It moved slightly up and down with every breath. I loved these tender movements of my head against her kind chest. For me it was the most secure place in the world. The rhythm of her beating heart was the music of my life and I often hummed my school rhymes while my head was on her chest. Both of us were watching the news on our tiny black and white television set. That was when the news flashed: *The infamous terrorist Akashdeep along with two of his accomplices has been shot down by CRPF jawans, yesterday. He killed nine jawans at Jagraon...*

Her chest stopped pulsating.

'Mommy!' I shouted.

'Mommy!' I cried.

She looked pale, her hands became chilled. I rushed to the kitchen wailing loudly and fetched a glass of water. That is what I had seen people doing in films in such a situation.

'Mommy...' I was still crying. I extended her the glass of water from my trembling tiny hands. She didn't take it. Tears flowed ceaselessly from my eyes. My legs were shaking and urine forced its way out. My mother's motionless eyes kept looking at the television set. I thought of God in panic. I thought of all my prayers during the morning assemblies.

'Annihilate the world but spare my mother,' I implored Him.

And then she breathed. And she cried bitterly. She clutched me into a hug and both of us cried. She cried in grief and I cried in relief. I believed in the power of prayer and continued doing it for some more days, my faith in God was reinforced.

The terrorists were besieged when they were sitting at a tubewell in village Rumi in Jagraon. It was Akashdeep's ancestral village. The informer was also accompanying the terrorists. One CRPF jawan got martyred in the combat.

The TV was still blaring and blurting. When the tide of tears relented a bit, I got up from my mother's lap and switched off the TV. She just sat there listlessly. She was drained of all energy. She went to her bed, lay down and continued sobbing into her pillow. I couldn't sleep because my father wasn't home as yet. I didn't expect her to get up and open the door for him. He came around 9:00 pm. He looked quite sad, not because Akashdeep had died, but because one of his customers had died. I had often heard him saying, 'Religion doesn't give you food. I am doing all this for money! To hell with their mission and their religion.'

'Shame on you… You have no right to call yourself a Sikh,' my mother used to retort with disdain.

'Yes, I am not a Sikh. I am a *Dalit*. Because I am still a *Dalit* so I am not a Sikh. Simply because there is no Sikhism as the Gurus had envisaged.' He would then go out of the house thumping his feet angrily.

At that time, I did not like my father's views, perhaps because they were not in consonance with my mother's. But eventually, I have come to the conclusion that he was more practical than my mother.

MADAM MOHINI - A Romantic Tale of Violence

After a few days, I mustered some courage and asked my mourning mother.

'Mommy, where did that uncle stay?' I asked so that she could let out some of her sorrow and feel relieved. It's always relieving to tell someone your sad story. This is the reason why I am talking to you too, Sukhbir.

So I asked my mother. She considered it for a while. Then she held my face with affection and kissed my forehead.

'His house was in the same village as mine.' She sighed and stared at the wall for a few minutes as if trying to read some writing on the wall.

She continued, 'We went to the same school. Since I was a girl, and that too a poor Dalit's daughter, I was taken out of school after class 10th but he continued his studies. He was a brilliant student, the most handsome boy in the whole village. He was the only son of his rich parents. He had a sister too. Though his father was a big landlord, he worked as a school teacher as well.

Akash took admission to Punjab Agriculture University, Ludhiana, to study veterinary science. He was doing very well in his studies. His only passion other than studies was guns. Those days, police spies took admission to various colleges and universities to spot militants who were working for the mission. There were some in his university, too.

One day, during lunch in the university mess, some boys started discussing AK 47 rifles, a Russian gun.

✦ 21 ✦

MADAM MOHINI - A Romantic Tale of Violence

Among those boys two were militants. Akash's technical knowledge about guns quietened them all. One of the militants did not like the superiority of his knowledge and flaunted, 'Oh keep quiet, have you ever seen an AK 47?'

'Though I have never seen one yet I can bet that I will put my finger on the trigger and fire as many rounds as you ask, neither less nor more,' Akash boasted to those boys.

His confidence was hurting the other boy.

'Alright, wait then,' The haughty boy left the mess, went to his room in the hostel, and brought one AK 47 rifle.

There was chaos in the mess and other boys started dispersing quickly. But Akash's fate held him there. He took the gun and fired some shots in the air. The news spread like wildfire on the campus. That evening, when he was going out of the university on his Yamaha-350, police officers were waiting for him at the gate because they were not allowed inside the campus. Yamaha-350 and Bullet Enfield bikes were banned by the government in those days. Akash panicked and ran back to the hostel leaving his bike behind. He didn't know what to do. In the meantime, police had picked up his father and tortured him. They beat the flesh off his ankle bones. He pleaded and cried for mercy but none came.'

My mother gave a long mournful pause.

'Akash was then left with no choice but to flee and join the mission. It was a point of no return for him.

MADAM MOHINI - A Romantic Tale of Violence

Thereafter, he planned various missions, all of which were intelligently crafted and flawlessly executed.'

I smiled feebly at my mother as all this didn't interest me much. I was keener to know about things between Akashdeep and her. But she cleverly, rather wisely, avoided that part of the story.

* * * * * * *

It was a very dark night – moonless and starless. Though many darker nights had yet to come, that one was the darkest of all that I had seen till then. All around people were getting killed. Anarchy was ruling the roost. Everyone seemed to be avenging their old and new rivals. Police officers were torturing innocents at the behest of the powerful and the rich. All unscrupulous, illegal, politically correct but ethically wrong acts of omission and commission were credited to the account of terrorists, who killed for their so-called cause. Punjab was plunged into the dark ages. Even ghosts were afraid of being outside on the roads and streets after dark. Shops were closed at 6:00 pm. A haunting silence would engulf the dark nights.

Do you think the dark age is over? Even I thought it was over. But it wasn't. Neither did the loot and killings stop. And we, I mean my party, will never let it end. We maintain an outer semblance of a bright age, but the inside has to remain dark. This is conducive for us, politicians.

MADAM MOHINI - A Romantic Tale of Violence

I was telling you about that dark night. That day, my father did not turn up. My mother held me in her lap and kept looking at the clock every minute.

'Mommy, please tell me a story,' I requested for the fourth time.

She looked extremely worried. She gently patted my head but couldn't utter a word. The clock struck the midnight hour. The bang of the clock startled her. She knew he was in trouble. I didn't know when I dozed off, peacefully hugging her. It was 1:00 am when she shook me violently. She saw the trouble coming. It was the police.

'Go!' She shrieked. 'Go... HIDE.' She pushed me.

I ran.

She ran after me and stopped me for a final second. She kneeled in front of me.

'Do you remember what you have to do now?' She spoke as fast as she could. I looked into her eyes. They were brimming with tears. She kissed me frantically and gave me a quick tight hug. My chest was pressed against her chest. Her heart was pounding fiercely.

'Yes, mommy.' I don't know how I managed to utter those words as my throat was choked and my body was trembling.

'Go then, my child,' and she pushed me towards the bedroom. In one corner of the room lay a ladder. I had to go up the ladder that reached a disguised shutter in one corner of the ceiling which opened outwards. I had

MADAM MOHINI - A Romantic Tale of Violence

to open that shutter and pull myself up on the roof. I did all that efficiently as I had practiced many times. Then I pushed the ladder away. It fell on the bedroom floor with a bang. Now I had to keep sitting there as quiet as a mouse.

I could hear sounds. BANG... CRASH... BOOM

'Listen, woman, tell us where he is?' a loud voice was demanding to know.

'How many times shall I tell you I DON'T KNOW...' my mom shouted.

'Aye... Keep your voice down,' one of the men screamed.

'*Saab*, she won't tell like this,' another voice said harshly.

'NO...leave... Leave me,' my mom was screaming. She wept aloud and kept saying, 'Please... Leave me.'

But no one seemed to pay heed. I wept quietly in impotent rage.

After half an hour, my mother's wailing became low and I heard one of the men saying, 'Let's take her along, *janab*.' He laughed jokingly, and so did the rest of the demons. My heart sank.

They drove away in their jeeps. The sounds of their jeeps gradually dissolved into a haunting silence. My chest tightened with foreboding. I cried and cried and waited for her to call or come to me. I peeped through the railing of the parapet and kept on staring at the street. I felt paralysed. My Mother's face which had

✦ 25 ✦

MADAM MOHINI - A Romantic Tale of Violence

been my first memory kept flashing before my blurred eyes. The wind was wailing in my ears. I turned to God, prayed, and begged. I closed my wet eyes and folded my hands. I recited all the prayers I had learned. But nothing happened. She didn't return. After infinite hours, the sun raised its ugly head. I went inside the house and started a fresh wait there. Evening came but she didn't come. I had cried too long to have tears anymore. Staying alone in the house without Mommy was a horrifying experience. But I had to. I was hungry. I ate the leftovers. After eating, my brain came up with an idea. I thought of striking a bargain with God and prayed again, 'If not mom, please send my daddy home.'

Though I had settled for the second choice, but it seemed God was too adamant and high-headed to relent. Neither of them returned. That was my last day with prayers. That was the last time I sought help from what people acclaim as GOD. I resorted to helping myself.

After another day of tormenting wait, I decided to go and look for her. I supposed that the police would have taken her to a police station. But which police station? I had no idea.

The next morning, I took my school bag and emptied it. Mom had hidden some money in one of the cupboards. I didn't know how much? But now I guess it would have been around five thousand rupees. I took all the money and kept it in my bag along with my

MADAM MOHINI - A Romantic Tale of Violence

favourite doll with the black shiny eyes. I came out of the house. I didn't forget to lock the main door, the way my mom did whenever we used to go out to buy things from the shop at the bend of the street.

Everyone in the neighbourhood knew that the police had taken my mother away. They probably also knew where my father had gone. But none of them came to help me. When my tiny feet were walking out of the street, their heads turned to look at me. I looked at them. The glare of my eyes was too much for them to endure and they looked away."

* * * * * * *

Chapter 2

"I shaded my eyes against the sun and looked lazily at the vast pooled fields of paddy. A flock of white cranes was busy picking worms and tadpoles in the fields. Their wings flashed against the bright green of the fields and the blue of the sky. A pair of eagles glided merrily wingtip to wingtip, round and round the fields looking for prey. One of them circled slowly, lower and lower, and executed a final sharp turn to scoop up a little snake and shoot up in the air again. The snake wriggled in its powerful claws. Some glittering droplets of water rolled off the snake's body. I felt a gush of warm sweat on my neck. What if the eagle flew over my head and the snake wriggled itself free right at that moment? I decided to run for shelter but before I could do that, the eagle soared high up into the sky.

It was a hot and sultry morning in July. The sun was matted by a thin layer of dust and clouds. Though its pallid light lacked lustre, it was hotter than ever. The air was absolutely still. My clothes clung to my

MADAM MOHINI - A Romantic Tale of Violence

sweating body. Heat pricked my skin like needles. I kept walking towards the city. My village 'Kauli' is about 19 kilometres from the city. The road, the roadside trees, the fields, the houses, everything looked weary, pale, and lousy."

Madam paused here for a long, deep sigh. The air in the room had turned melancholy and sad. Sukhbir looked at her intently, deeply interested in what would be coming next in her story.

"Though buses were plying, I didn't know which one to catch. So, I walked for more than three hours which seemed no less than eternity. I reached Punjabi University, which sits on the outskirts of the city. I thought of asking someone the way to the police station. There were so many people around. Everyone looked malevolent and I was scared. Mom had told me that the times were full of wild wolves and a girl was never safe outside without mommy or daddy. But she didn't tell me what should a girl do if both mommy and daddy are lost. I had to fend for myself and needed to take help of the kindest looking person.

'Uncle, where is the police station?' I politely asked a tall old man with a flowing grey beard. He wore a saffron turban, the colour which my father wore. This saffron turban phenomenon was a queer one. In those days they were widely worn. Some said they were a guard against the wrath of militants, some said it implied that the wearer supported the mission.

MADAM MOHINI - A Romantic Tale of Violence

The man looked at me through the thick lenses of his glasses. His eyeballs appeared double in size. They flicked from side to side.

'Are you alone?' he asked in a very low voice.

'No, my mommy...' I didn't even complete the sentence when the old man spoke again.

'Are you mad? Go back.' And he scampered away.

I walked a few steps. A little boy was dribbling a ball just outside a petrol pump.

'Do you know where the police station is?' I asked him.

The boy tossed the ball up and down for a while and then flicked a thumb over his shoulder pointing towards the south direction. That meant I had to keep walking down the road for some more miles. In those days, there were not many buildings on either side of the road. That was a newly developing area with lots of vacant plots and a few half-constructed houses. I had travelled on this road before, whenever mommy and I took a bus to Jagraon. We had to take a local bus from our village to the Patiala bus stand and from there we had to take a big bus to Jagraon.

I was too tired to take even a step further. My feet had developed blisters and the heat in the air burnt my eyes. I thought of hiring a rickshaw. After a while, I saw a rickshaw coming. I urgently motioned my hand and it stopped.

'I want to go to the police station,' I told the rickshaw puller.

+ 30 +

MADAM MOHINI - A Romantic Tale of Violence

He was a dark lanky Bihari with hollowed cheeks and mysterious eyes. He paused to look at me for a long time before asking, '*Paisa hai?* (Do you have money?),'in a deadpan voice.

'Yes,' I replied.

'*Das rupeeya lagega.* (I will charge ten rupees.),' he looked at me questioningly, as if doubting my word.

'*Das rupeeya?*' I was taken aback.

It was a lot of money. I knew he was charging double than normal but I was just not able to walk anymore. Though I had money with me, it was not to be squandered on luxuries. But I had no option as I was too tired. I had heard that the police did anything you wanted as long as you pay them under the table. It was a vital piece of practical knowledge. A policeman's apoplectic eyes, a mouth full of indigenous abuses, and a brisk under-the-table business could be attributed to the prevalence of the 'dark age'. But how he sustained all that effectively till today is a stark example of self-sustaining professionalism. But I tell you, these poor cops are a misunderstood lot.

The rickshaw puller took me to the nearest police station. A big arched board outside the building said 'Thana Sadar Patiala'. My nervous little feet walked inside. A grim atmosphere prevailed but the place was abuzz with activity. Two constables at the gate were seemed to be involved in an idle conversation. I walked up to them.

'Police uncle, is my mommy here?' I asked in a trembling voice. The apprehension of hearing a 'no' made my heartbeat really fast.

'Aye girl, go home.' One of the constables answered in the harshest voice that I had ever heard. Something from my ribcage dived down to my belly and something from my belly rose up to hit my throat. It hurt. My eyes pooled. I am sure my face looked lifeless and scared.

'Police uncle...' It took me a lot to utter this. Two tears rolled out of my eyes.

'What?' he was harsh again.

'Uncle...my mommy...I have money...' my voice was breaking and incoherent. I was unable to complete my sentences.

The cops exchanged a quick glance. One of them kneeled in front of me. He was a changed man now; he suddenly turned polite.

'What is her name?' he asked me nicely.

I wiped my eyes quickly. A flash of hope lit my face and I replied instantly, 'Ranjit Kaur'.

'How much money do you have?' he was even politer.

I swiftly lowered my bag and opened its buckles to show him the money. His eyes glinted.

'Close it...close it...' His tone had an air of urgency and secrecy about it. His head turned to the other constable and their eyes met. The other cop nodded.

'Come with me, daughter, and tell me more about your mother and how did she come here?' He kept his

MADAM MOHINI - A Romantic Tale of Violence

hand gently on my shoulder guiding me to one side of the room. Sobbing, I told him the whole story. He listened attentively, considered for a while, and then asked in a voice overladen with sympathy.

'Do you have other members in your family like uncles, aunts, or grandparents?'

'No, only my Nana-Nani (maternal grandparents).' I was still sobbing.

'Where do they stay?' he asked me gently.

'Village Rumi,' I replied through my tears.

'The one near Jagraon?' he asked hesitantly.

I nodded in agreement.

'Ok...'

He looked around cautiously and said really sweetly, 'Don't worry. Think of me as your uncle only and do as I say.'

I nodded. My tear-stained cheeks felt sticky and slime was crawling out of my nostrils.

'Do you have anything else in your bag?' he whispered.

'Yes, my doll and keys...' I wiped the slime with the sleeve of my frock.

'Right, come with me,' he told me softly.

He hired an auto-rickshaw and took me to the main bus stand. He made me sit in a Rumi-bound bus and bought me a ticket.

'Now listen, go to your Nana–Nani's house. I will free your mommy and tell her to come there. Don't

◆ 33 ◆

MADAM MOHINI - A Romantic Tale of Violence

talk to any strangers and never tell anyone that you are alone,' he wagged his finger at me.

'Are you sure, uncle?' I asked in a languid voice.

'Yes, trust me.' His voice was low but crisp. 'Now give me your bag.'

I gave it. He took out my doll, keys, and a Rupee hundred bill and gave them to me. Then he rushed off the bus. I watched him through the window of the bus, thanking him for his kindness. At that moment, I believed that everyone was not bad and there were good people as well. I continued to believe this till the time I realised that not everyone is a wild wolf, looking for opportunities to rape, some were clever foxes, looking for opportunities to cheat.

I reached the village in the evening. Even though the evening was paler than the day but it was as hot as the day had been. As soon as I alighted from the bus full of gloomy faces, I heard wails — heart-rending wails. They came from every direction. The village was drowned in a sea of blood-curdling sounds. I started running towards my Nani's house. I immediately needed shelter in her lap. I wanted to dig my head in her bosom and cover my ears with her *dupatta* so that I could not hear those frightening sounds. I cringed in panic.

It took me just about three minutes to reach the house as it was not very far from the bus stand, but those three minutes seemed like an eternity. While I was running, I wished those minutes would shrink into

MADAM MOHINI - A Romantic Tale of Violence

seconds but as soon as those minutes ended, I wished they had never ended. What I saw was worse than what I was running from. A group of villagers was huddled in a circle in the compound of my Nana-Nani's house. They were having whispered consultations. I hurried to the pack of onlookers and pushed my way through them. In the centre of the circle lay two white sheets, covering something which seemed like two bodies. An old woman saw me. She rushed towards me, gripped me in her hug, and started crying aloud.

Then she suddenly paused and asked, 'Where is your mommy?' I was too panicked to utter a word but her question gave me a huge relief as it implied that my mother was surely not under one of those white sheets. Another woman came to me. She knelt beside me and curled her arm around my shoulder. I knew her. She was my mommy's friend, Mani. She explained to me that my Nana-Nani had been killed. I couldn't cry. The shock was so ill-timed and immense that my frazzled eyes turned dry. I was too numb to even understand what she was saying. She was telling me that my Nana-Nani were coming back from Ludhiana yesterday by train when their train was intercepted by terrorists. One hundred and twenty people had been killed on that train. Sixty of them were from this village. Almost every house in the village was wailing that day.

I had never ever seen such a harrowing spectre. Living people were soaked in tears and sweat and the dead

✦ 35 ✦

MADAM MOHINI - A Romantic Tale of Violence

in blood. There was a lot of hysterical activity at the cremation ground for the next two days. One group of mourners would leave after cremating a body and the other group would enter. Every available pair of hands was busy arranging the final journey of the dead. Sixty earthen pitchers were broken and their water created a slush outside the cremation ground. My Nana-Nani had also perished. I saw their once moving; eating; laughing and praying bodies, turn into ashes and gases. The village air was reeking of burning flesh and bones.

The place and the house changed, the rest of everything remained the same for me. My mommy's friend Mani, slept with me for some nights. She also waited for my mother with me. She felt that she could not leave me alone. I spent most of the day just sitting and looking at the main door. Every minute encapsulated a hope that the door would open and my mommy would rush in to hug me. I imagined her around the corner eagerly coming home to me. Every time the sound of a growling bus engine emerged the hope became stronger. The sound would move nearer and nearer. Then it would stop moving for a minute; the rickety door of the bus would open and close with a bang and then it would move away. And my waiting heart would grow keener. But she didn't turn up. *Why was the police uncle taking so long?* I wondered.

Two weeks passed but my hope didn't relent and I didn't give up. Mani's husband, Gurpal, who was working in Delhi, came to take her along.

MADAM MOHINI - A Romantic Tale of Violence

'How can I go leaving her alone? She is just a kid,' she told her husband in a voice full of concern for me.

'But how long can you wait for Ranjit?' he asked emphatically.

'The girl is quite confident that she would come,' Mani told her husband.

'Come on! How can she know? Moreover, this place has become a hell. Do you see how people are being killed indiscriminately, day in and day out? Chaos and anarchy...' He clenched his fists and shook them in disgust. 'You leave home in the morning but you can never be sure of making back alive at night.'

'I know all this.' Mani dropped her eyes.

She wiped her tearful eyes with the edge of her *dupatta*. No words passed between them for the next few minutes. Suddenly, a low murmur buzzed through the evening air. A sound of water drops trickling somewhere could be heard. I sighed behind the shut door and cried quietly. A breeze gushed in through the window and stirred my frock. The breeze had a smell of moisture in it which meant it was raining somewhere near. The idea of imminent rain distracted my mind for a while but the tears and the helplessness came back soon.

'Mommy, come back...' I uttered to myself in grief.

'Alright, wait if you must but not for more than a week,' Gurpal said after a few seconds.

I think she would have smiled. I couldn't decide how to react. It seemed I had lost all feelings. I was neither

✦ 37 ✦

MADAM MOHINI - A Romantic Tale of Violence

happy nor sad. Gurpal's family stayed at Jagraon, hardly fifteen minutes from our village. We had to go there and stay overnight. In the morning, Gurpal had to leave for Delhi and we would then come back to my Nana-Nani's house to wait for my mother. It was already 5:00 pm and we had to hurry as the dark was too dark those days. We took the last bus and reached Jagraon at 5:30 pm.

The bazaar was emptying quickly, the merchants finishing their haggling for the day and closing their shops. We picked our way through the dwindling crowd. Shutters of the shops were being downed one after the other. Mani and Gurpal walked fast and I trotted behind, trying to keep pace with them. On reaching their home, an old lady, perhaps Gurpal's mother, opened the door.

'Look at the watch. You know these are bad times,' she chided the couple mildly. They didn't reply. Soon she noticed me. She eyed me up and down.

'Who is she?' she smiled at me and I smiled back.

'She is my friend Rani's daughter. Rani is missing. She is staying with me till the time her mother is found,' Mani rested her hand on my head.

The smile on the old woman's face wilted and a frown appeared on her forehead.

'That means she is from the sweeper caste?' she asked in a hardened tone.

'How does it matter?' Mani's voice was a little louder.

✦ 38 ✦

MADAM MOHINI - A Romantic Tale of Violence

'It might not matter to you,' she turned to Gurpal and continued, 'but ours is a family of repute. Tell your wife to throw the girl out,' she ordered him tersely.

'She is not going anywhere,' shouted Mani.

'Do you want to pollute the whole house? If she is not going, I am going,' the old woman replied giving an ultimatum.

This was the perfect time for Gurpal to intervene.

'Where would she go at this hour, she is a little girl,' he spoke calmly and took some steam out of the situation. The old lady looked away. He turned to Mani.

'Listen, can we make her sleep on the veranda tonight?' Mani looked away too.

I just stood there, listening to they discuss me as if I was not present.

But finally, he succeeded in extracting an agreement from the belligerent parties which meant for me a night on the veranda on a string cot without a fan above or a mattress below. I lay there in the darkness. The jute strings of the cot were hurting my skin. I was close to tears. I missed my mom and just wanted to sit in her lap. I started thinking about the good police uncle and clung to the hope that he had given me. I thought about all the good times which seemed to be just as many steps away from me as my mommy was. The stillness of the air was disturbed by a steady breeze. It felt cooler as I was wet with sweat. A rumble of thunder rolled

✦ 39 ✦

MADAM MOHINI - A Romantic Tale of Violence

in the sky and a cloud growled somewhere. The much-awaited monsoon had arrived!

My heart cheered when the drops of rain kissed my face. The breeze quickly rustled up to fan away the heat. I always loved the rain. I could never make out why people ran for shelter when it rained. Are those people made up of salt? I never ran. Even my mother, unlike other mothers, allowed me to bathe in the rain. The monsoon sows what the earth reaps. The barrenness of the plain gets seeded with the lushness of green. The breeze caresses the airy bags of water and applies its moist fingers along the heat wilted curves of the saplings. New leaves are born, a colourful bloom springs forth and under the dark brooding canopy, happy activity begins. As the showers start, the drains choke with excitement and tiny rivulets reinvent their dry beds.

Those were the days when I enjoyed every luscious drop of rain. But now people don't let me. As soon as it rains heavily, the canals breach their banks and the constituencies get inundated. Instead of enjoying the rain-induced songs of the birds, we hear the grumblings and groanings of the homeless angry people. How is it our fault if the drains get choked with excitement and the canals breach with merriment? The excitement which chokes the drains reaches them after exchanging many hands. Ultimately, the common man himself is responsible for his civic miseries. We don't tell them

MADAM MOHINI - A Romantic Tale of Violence

to use plastic bags. Of course, some governments have banned them but in Punjab, we don't take such drastic steps. We are not irresponsible to ruin the livelihood of those running the plastic bag factories and the ones employed in them. This would be immoral. The industrialist is our friend. The bigger the entrepreneur, the stronger is the bond that we forge with him. As for the environment, it won't take a turn for the worst before the next election."

Madam looked at Sukhbir. He was visibly amused by all this.

"I will tell you an incident," Madam laughed lightly. "You know, Sukhbir, when I was a novice in this field, I was quite foolishly credulous. Once an environmentalist came to me and started telling me about the disastrous consequences of tube-well irrigation, 'Madam underground water is receding fast — 60 cm a year! Can you imagine? 60 cm a year! Try and think what would our Punjab be like without groundwater?' His face was almost ripping apart with worry.

'I don't know,' Pat came my cold reply.

'We are causing desertification of our state. Our eyes would yearn for greenery but we won't get to see any,' he told me with passion.

I too was alarmed by the thought. 'What to do then?' I asked with my eyes open wide.

'Madam, we should harvest our rainwater. We should make it mandatory,' his hand movements indicated urgency.

✦ 41 ✦

MADAM MOHINI - A Romantic Tale of Violence

'Ok, I will talk to CM *sahib*.' I sounded impressed and he smiled complacently as if he had accomplished a mission. So, I took an appointment with CM *sahib* and reached his bungalow the same evening.

'*Sahib*, there is an emergency.' I took off like this.

'Emergency?' He was as calm as ever.

'Sir, our groundwater is depleting and soon our state will become a desert,' I explained quickly, quoting the environmentalist.

'Will the waters stay for the next five years?' He was amazingly calm.

'Of course, yes.' I replied with confidence.

'Then no need to bother and panic. Anything else?' He said dismissively.

And I walked out of his office feeling like a stupid over-enthusiast."

Sukhbir and Madam laughed together making small sounds like pebbles striking each other. Then she continued with her narration.

"So, that night on the string cot, when it started raining, I kept lying in the rain. It was soothing and cutting prickly heat. My mother always allowed me to be in the rain but she herself never ventured out of the shade. Instead, she would shower instructions from her shelter. I would face up or face down on the cemented floor as she willed. After satisfying herself that I had sufficiently exposed my heat-affected parts to the curative rain, she would go into the kitchen. A cup

MADAM MOHINI - A Romantic Tale of Violence

of hot tea with ginger, cardamom, and a dash of black pepper was mandatory after my session in the rain. Onion and potato *pakoras* with mint *chutney*, however, provided the real incentive for gulping down the brew.

A clap of thunder startled me out of my reverie. Lightening threw a flash and the wet cemented floor of the veranda was illuminated for a moment. Something roared again. This time, it was not thunder. The earth shook a little and I heard the rat-a-tat-tat of gunfire close by. I saw a dark silhouette hobbling frantically across the street. A white light flashed, lit the sky in silver. It flashed again and was followed by a rapid staccato of gunfire.

I yelped and sprang to my feet and raced towards the rooms. I banged my fists on one door after another but none opened. Somewhere a glass shattered and someone shouted. I ran towards the back lawn looking for shelter. My foot slipped on the wet floor and I fell flat on my back with my hands outstretched. I hurriedly got onto my feet again. A cluster of clay pots was lying outside the windows of one of the rooms. Without thinking and in panic, I just jumped and fitted myself into the space between the pots. I wrapped my arms around myself. It continued to rain. The pitter-patter of the rain provided a faint background sound. A siren went off in the distance. I was crying, tears streaming down my face. I stayed huddled there until the early hours of the morning, too scared to even move. The

MADAM MOHINI - A Romantic Tale of Violence

shootings and explosions lasted less than an hour but they frightened me badly.

Just before sunrise, the rain stopped. I heard some voices through the window under which I was sitting.

'No way... This is an insane place. We have got to leave immediately and the sooner you leave this girl, the better it is. I don't want to get sucked into this whirlpool of violence,' Gurpal was saying.

'Listen carefully. I need to talk about it,' said Mani calmly. 'Let's take the girl along,' she added.

'Are you mad?' said Gurpal.

'Listen, dear, she told me that the police have taken her mother. The newspaper said that the police seized weapons from their house and her father had absconded. Police have not declared her mother's arrest. That means the chances of Rani's return are very low. The girl has nowhere to go,' Mani was trying to convince Gurpal, but he seemed unconvinced. 'And one more thing,' Mani tried to convince him again, 'the girl is the sole heir to the properties of her grandparents as well as of her parents. If she stays with us, we can get all those properties.'

There was silence for some moments. I guessed Mani's argument had finally convinced Gurpal. As it turned out, I never got a chance to know if Mani really didn't know that I didn't have any property if she actually had an eye on my property which she imagined I had or it was just an empty argument to lure Gurpal into taking me with them.

MADAM MOHINI - A Romantic Tale of Violence

After a few hours, I was again walking behind Mani and Gurpal. We crossed the residential streets and trekked through a barren patch of rough land that led to the bus stop. Last night's rain had left everything drenched and muddy. The morning was grey and the sky overcast. The air was dense and damp. The *peepals,* acacias, and banyans looked darker and deeper than usual, casting unnatural shadows. We hopped onto a New Delhi-bound bus and sat cramped with other passengers. The bus was packed to the gills. Two passengers sitting on the seat behind us were discussing last night's gunfire.

'A group of terrorists attacked the police station,' said one.

'How do they dare so much?' said the other in a controlled voice.

'If these mother fucker political leaders want, the problem can be solved in a day. Life has become so uncertain,' the first voice sounded agitated.

'All this is created by these politicians only,' the second voice said with contempt.

'You are right. It was only after the politicians discovered Bhindranwale's popularity that they began to flatter him; the hubris entered the soul of this rustic preacher and he became arrogant and overbearing,' the first voice replied with disdain.

'Speak low, do you want to be killed?' said the second voice, getting alarmed by the sudden statement.

'What is this living? Every day I live in fear —fear of losing my son, fear of losing my life. This fear is already killing me,' the first voice sounded devastated.

'Keep the faith, things will become fine one day,' the second voice tried to console him.

'Nothing will be fine,' chided the first voice. His body seemed to tremble. 'The politicians are cooking their broth on the fire in which our bones are burning. They are using Bhindranwale as a pawn in the game of their dirty party politics,' he breathed heavily. 'This Giani and Darbara, they call themselves Punjabis? Chee! They are just watching their own political interests,' he snuffed with disgust.

'Come on, keep your voice low, please,' the second voice was suppressed and fearful. I could hear his teeth grit.

But the first man got further agitated. 'The Gandhis at the centre are also trying to encash his political potential. Who will lose in this game? Can anyone tell me who will lose?' The first man was standing now and speaking loudly. Then he burst into tears.

The other man thought it better to disown him. His verbosity could cost him dear. Such a public vent to your outrage against the system was not devoid of danger and he was scared for his life.

The first man cried for some time and then resorted to mumbling. Then he fell quiet. No one dared to sit with him for the rest of the journey. Nobody wanted to be associated with him in any way.

I wanted to turn around to look at that man but Gurpal had strictly ordered not to do that. I tried to hear other conversations. I do not remember much of it except a woman's pitiful voice saying, 'Poor man! He seemed to be mentally unhinged. Not his fault, anyone can go insane if his young son gets killed.'

The bus wheeled its way on the National Highway-1 — the historical Grand Trunk Road which has been there for ages. I stuck my head outside the window. The moist wind flapped against my face with such a force that I had to make an effort to keep my eyes open. The tiny drops of rain soothed my face and felt comfortable. But slowly the drizzle turned into a downpour and the drops stung my face. I pulled my head inside. I licked the drops of rain that trailed down my lips. The bus crossed the Shambhu barrier and entered the state of Haryana. I continued watching out of the window through the haze of rain. Nothing changed — the landscape, the weather, the vegetation, the sprawling bright green paddy fields, and the smell of the moist air mixed with diesel fumes. The only difference was that even though here too, Sikhs could be seen in sufficient numbers but that queer saffron turban was conspicuous by its absence.

* * * * * * *

MADAM MOHINI - A Romantic Tale of Violence

It was evening. The bus entered New Delhi. From a mofussil town in the dusty lap of Punjab to New Delhi felt like a big leap. There were buses, auto-rickshaws, and yellow-black cabs all along the road. The traffic rules were equally run over by this motley procession of vehicles, as it was in Punjab, each one charting its own path with utter disdain for the others on the road. The vehicles were spilling over with people who were not only packed inside but also hung from doors and were even mounted on roofs. Everybody seemed to be running from gunshots to the haven of our glorious nation's capital, the showcase of our secular republic. I goggled out of the window. I could see never-ending wide roads flanked by infinite buildings. Scores of sullen homeless people spread on the pavements spoiled the whole showcase. I felt I was passing through a wormhole and travelling to the future. Here, everything looked bright except the air which was full of fumes of diesel and petrol mixed with dust. It smelt foul and my nostrils burnt. Nevertheless, it was glamorous. New Delhi never lost its lustre.

An auto-rickshaw farted its way through the roads of Delhi. We were sitting in it. Every road it took was narrower than the previous one and eventually, it reached a very tight street overlooked by many stories of pigeon holes, which were called apartments. We had reached Mansarovar Park in Shahadra. Mani and Gurpal lived in one of the apartments here. As

✦ 48 ✦

MADAM MOHINI - A Romantic Tale of Violence

we entered the apartment, Gurpal felt happy and relieved.

'Ah! I feel good here,' said Gurpal. He took off his turban and scratched his head. 'Teach her household work.' He glanced at me and then looked knowingly at Mani.

Mani nodded in agreement.

'How safe!' He breathed deeply, looking content.

He did not know at that time that safety is determined by the ones who rule you. This is how it works in our country. The ones who are found responsible for jeopardizing the safety of citizens are absolved for being a part of the mob. What can a government do to a mob? A mob has no body and no mind of its own. Yet, all of them fail to camouflage as a mob. Those are the ones who get caught and are tried in the court of law. And our law takes its own steady pace. Perfectly appropriate, after all, slow and steady wins the race."

Madam sighed... Suddenly, there was a knock at the door. Sukhbir went to open it. A servant stood outside with a tray of tea and snacks. He came in, poured the tea, and handed a cup to Madam. She took a sip and shouted, 'What is this? You call it tea!' She pushed the cup away on the table. Her face flushed red and her upper lip quivered. The servant, a young Nepali, stood with folded hands. He dared not utter a word. She glanced at him briefly and started striding up and down the room.

MADAM MOHINI - A Romantic Tale of Violence

This was not new to Sukhbir. Of late, she often had these mood swings and Sukhbir bore them gracefully. He would always listen dutifully for he knew that her anger was like a flash of lightning. It would go off before you even realised it. She often pounced on Sukhbir but he evaded her ire with his 'matter of fact' brief syllables. He remembered how she had reacted when he called her up late one night just before the last assembly polls.

'Hello, Madam,' Sukhbir's voice was trembling.

'What Madam? I was with you an hour ago. I have told you a thousand times to make a list of the points you want to discuss. As soon as my mind starts getting a little peace... Anyway, what is so important that you are calling me now?' She answered with irritation in her voice.

'Madam, I am sorry. It is regarding tomorrow's rally. Madam, I just wanted to ask which liquor is to be distributed.' Sukhbir asked her hesitantly.

'Of course, *Desi* (country liquor). What a stupid thing to ask! What do you think, should we serve them with scotch?' She replied disdainfully.

'No...no...I mean...' Sukhbir stammered.

'What I mean... Voters are not trustworthy anymore. Those days of yore have gone when they swore by gurus and voted sincerely for the one who gave them liquor, money, or *bhukki* (poppy husk). Their moral values have depleted. They don't hesitate to enjoy the parties thrown by your opponents. And ultimately whom will

✦ 50 ✦

MADAM MOHINI - A Romantic Tale of Violence

they vote remains a secret because of this sucking secret ballot.' She vented, giving an explanation for her choice.

'Yes, Madam.' Sukhbir agreed with her.

'In the last parliamentary elections, did I tell you what happened?' She continued.

'No...' A sluggish 'no' was quickly followed by a reconsidered yes. 'Yes, Madam.'

'I don't think I told you. (Madam cut him off) Dalbir Batal Ji was contesting against Ishmeet Singh for the Lok Sabha seat from Faridkot constituency. Now our Batal Sahib is a very naive man. He generously distributed money, liquor, and bhukki among the voters. No stinginess was shown. On the other hand, that shameless Ishmeet simply floated a slogan —

Dalbir de note (take money from Dalbir)
Ishmeet nu vote (and vote for Ishmeet)

This sounded impressive to all those illiterate stupid voters and they voted for Ishmeet. These voters threw away all rules of propriety.'

'Yes, Madam,' Sukhbir nodded.

'But what to do? Huh... We have no choice but to feed them,' Madam questioned him mockingly.

'Yes, Madam,' Sukhbir again just nodded. There was nothing that he could add to that.

'Anything else?' She asked him.

'No, Madam.'

MADAM MOHINI - A Romantic Tale of Violence

Sukhbir could feel that by the end of any such session of rebuke everything would be back to normal. But she was still unhappy with the bad tea.

'Cheh!' she uttered. She shook her head with what seemed more of helplessness than disdain. She went to the cupboard in the corner, opened it and squatted in front of it on the floor. In the lowest section of the cupboard lay a wooden rectangular box, hidden behind a pile of clothes. She took out the box. It was made of walnut wood with stunning golden inlaid patterns of snakes on its lid. Two magnificent cobras stood face-to-face with their raised hoods. Their ruby eyes flashed fire. Softly, she ran her hand over the box. She opened it and took out a doll wearing a red silk frock. The doll stared mutely into her eyes. Madam's face began to twitch. An old memory raised the hair on her arms. After a while, her shoulders gradually relaxed. She shut her eyes. The silence of the air was stirred by the hoot of a train on one of the tracks which criss-crossed the landscape of Patiala.

* * * * * * *

Chapter 3

At this hour of the day, the city is bursting with sounds, the shouts of vendors mingled with the blare of Punjabi music, the spluttering rickshaws, and the jingling bells of temples. Gurbani blaring out of Gurudwaras. An intricate network of streets, ranging from the width of a bicycle to that of a six-wheeled truck, intersecting each other here and there, thereby dividing the city into many localities. Some of these localities are congested and overpopulated and some spacious and underpopulated. Far from the cramped tiny sweet shops, meat shops, busy *dhabas*, tightly jammed roads, and away from the maddening crowd of ordinary people, sat a magnificent bungalow, painted in red and white. A well-kept vast garden ran along all sides of the bungalow. The sprawling lawns on both sides of the broad driveway looked even more alluring in the bright sun. The metalled driveway was as shiny as the night sky.

MADAM MOHINI - A Romantic Tale of Violence

She sat at one of the windows which overlooked the garden of that house. Sunlight slanted in and cast a triangular wedge of light on the Kashmiri rug on the floor.

"Can you see this tree?" She pointed to the mulberry tree in the garden. Sukhbir craned his neck to glance out.

"There was one like this behind our house in the village and it had the juiciest mulberries." She then stared out of the window, at the sun-stained tree, seemingly lost in the past.

"You know, in our village, there was a pond of rippling water which sometimes looked blue and sometimes green. Beyond that pond, at the farthest edge of the village, there were the sun swept *tibbas*, where the cobras mated at night or so my mother told me. Wild hares lived around those *tibbas*. My mother never allowed me to go near them. However, I was allowed to go to the pond. I often waded in its shallow end. Alarmed, tiny grey toads would hop out of my way, while the water would lap at my shins. The gleam of the pond's surface was broken every now and then, by some movement from the underlying fishes." She kept on looking out of the window, staring into nothingness. Then she cleared her throat and continued.

"Throughout my days in Delhi, I carried on waiting for some news of my mom. I waited to receive either a verbal message or a letter from Punjab which would say

MADAM MOHINI - A Romantic Tale of Violence

that my mother was back and would be coming to take me along. I always kept my things packed and ready so that I could move immediately if my mother arrived uninformed. Days turned into months. I continued working as a servant in Mani's house. She was kind to me but Gurpal was quite rude. Gradually his rudeness started getting interluded by mildly honeyed words whenever Mani was out of the home. His eyes would dance up and down my body. It started making me feel uncomfortable and I tried to stay away from him as much as was possible. But he didn't dare to attempt anything more than sly staring, perhaps, owing to the deterrence created by my parents' suspected links with the militants. It was said that the Militants never spared anyone who molested girls/women. This was one bright streak of the otherwise 'Dark Age', which saved me from becoming a rape victim.

Winter came out of its slumber and stretched her body. Her icy-cold breath slowly replaced the comfortable autumn air. My hands would become numb. I could not feel them every time I washed clothes or cleaned the dishes. I watched the chilled clear night skies and often talked to the stars which blinked at me. Then came spring for a short time followed by the sizzling summer of 1984.

The area where we were staying was a warm working-class neighbourhood. Families from different states and different religions lived together happily. Our

MADAM MOHINI - A Romantic Tale of Violence

next-door neighbour was one Mohinder Singh, a Hindu from Haryana, whose wife Radha always shared sweets with us that she had cooked. In turn, Mani offered her the special dishes cooked in our kitchen. Mohinder and Gurpal would go together for evening walks while Mani and Radha gossiped. Radha was a homely wife who was turning fat on schedule after having two children, both boys; whereas, Mani was a tall and slim *sardarni*. But they enjoyed talking about anything and everything.

May was about to end. I was chopping onions in the kitchen. There was some tension in the air. Mohinder and Gurpal looked serious and seemed to be discussing something grave sitting in the living room. I stopped chopping, took a broom and began sweeping the drawing-room floor. I edged closer and closer to them, trying to hear what they were discussing.

'But the army is meant to protect the country's frontiers, not to fight its own people,' Gurpal sounded agitated.

'Perhaps, violence could be curbed like this. She claims that Sikh temples have been converted into fortresses by the extremists,' Mohinder tried to pacify him.

'You don't know, Mohinder, what dirty politics are being played. Putting Punjab under the military rule will not solve any problem. You will see!' Gurpal said emphatically.

'As per the radio about 70,000 army men have been posted at strategic points, in and around Amritsar. It

MADAM MOHINI - A Romantic Tale of Violence

is possible that the army might be able to bring the militants to heel and peace may return,' Mohinder said thoughtfully.

But Gurpal continued to look worried. I prayed, don't know to whom, for the safety of my mother. Actually, we Indians are habitual prayer mutterers. It just happens spontaneously as if it is coded in our genes.

A few days later, Karamjit Singh came to Mani's house. He was her cousin and a captain in the Sikh regiment posted at Agra. His wife was in Sangrur, in Punjab and was about to deliver a baby. So he had taken leave to join her. He had to take a train from Delhi but when he reached here, he came to know that all rail, road, and air services to Punjab had been suspended. That is why he came to stay with Mani till the time the services would be resumed. The entry of foreigners into Punjab had also been banned. I did not know why all this was being done.

It was Karamjit's second day with us. He would go to the market every third hour to try to contact his family by phone. However, every time he returned frustrated. All phone lines were dysfunctional. He was dying of anxiety. After one of his trips to the market, I saw him scrambling up the stairs while I was drying out the laundry on the tiny balcony. He hurried inside the house. I sensed something seriously wrong and swiftly followed him in.

✦ 57 ✦

MADAM MOHINI - A Romantic Tale of Violence

'Mani... Mani...' and an involuntary groan escaped his lips.

Mani came running. 'What happened?'

'All is ruined.' He fell to his knees and started crying. A heartbeat later, with a surge of rage, an all-consuming blistering fury he screamed, 'They will repent!'

Mani got restless. 'What happened, *veer?*' she shouted. 'Please tell me. Is *bhabhi* alright?' She kneeled in front of him and shook him by his shoulders. Strange foreboding gave her goosebumps. He tried to control his tears and answered, 'I don't know what is happening to my family'. He was panting. 'Punjab is under curfew. The army has attacked Harmandir Sahib.' The pain in his chest was so intense that for an instant it looked that his heart had stopped beating.

'What?' Mani clamped her hand to her mouth. She was shocked. 'How do you know?'

'I heard people talking.' His voice sounded cracked.

'It could be a rumour; this cannot happen. Indira Gandhi is a seasoned Prime Minister. She can't let this happen.' Mani seemed to be reassuring herself more than him.

'This is no rumour. They have devastated the temple complex and killed Bhindranwale and his men. After this, I don't think the Sikhs should either live in India or with India.' He seemed to be completely rattled.

'No self-respecting Sikh will condone this desecration of Harmandir Sahib,' Mani said with her eyes clouding with pain. 'Veer, calm down.' She sighed inwardly.

✦ 58 ✦

MADAM MOHINI - A Romantic Tale of Violence

'I am resigning from the services of this government.' His voice turned resolute. He rose shakily to his feet, his breath coming in short sharp bursts.

I realised that something disastrous had happened to the Sikhs but could not figure out the extent of the disaster. It was only after some days when more news from Punjab started pouring in that the things started becoming clearer. All India Radio and Doordarshan were strangely quiet about the disaster. It was only BBC radio which kept us abreast of what supposedly was happening in Punjab. The Army had destroyed the temple with bullets and bombs. Bodies of women and children were seen to be floating in the sacred pool for many days. The precincts were reeking with the stench of death and cordite. Even as a child, I knew that this won't be forgiven. This was sacrilege.

As he had resolved, Karamjit resigned from the army and vowed to avenge the rape of the most sacred temple of the Sikhs. When services were resumed, he left for Sangrur. He was declared an absconding soldier. I never met him again.

The days went by as anticipated. Though breathing eased and the fever abated, the lips of the wound didn't pull together. The rains were early and especially perverse that year, washing away the first tender buds of roses that had shyly begun to grow on the rose bushes planted in a pot on the balcony. I had patiently been watering it every evening and was waiting to see it bloom.

MADAM MOHINI - A Romantic Tale of Violence

Clouds hunched beetle-browed over Delhi. Nobody, it seemed, even remembered when they had last seen the sun. There were short breaks in the downpour. Barely would a bedraggled sparrow shake out its plumage and begin to warble then the deluge would begin again. The placid river Yamuna which skirted Delhi had turned into a swollen roaring monster.

Whenever distressing thoughts crossed my mind, I would open the window and look at the rain. Mani didn't like to have the windows opened. I would carefully open the windows, barely a scratch, to let in the fresh moisture-rich air. I would squat on the floor, dampness dancing on my skin until Mani would pass by and slap the window shut with a sharp cry of impatience.

'What are you doing lingering by the window? Who will go and buy vegetables for dinner?' She would rebuke me.

I would sheepishly scurry off. The wind would keep beating its palms against the window shutter.

Finally, the monsoon ended. The rattling of the rain on the concrete ended and a watery sun blinked. The rain had softened the air and it was now filled with bird calls. Cuckoos and bulbuls skipped through the trees and skimmed the rooftops with their throats swelled with melody. Autumn stepped in. I kept thinking about the lush green fields of paddy that would have grown tall and thick back home. I missed having seen it ripening into gold under the autumn sun the farmers, getting

✦ 60 ✦

MADAM MOHINI - A Romantic Tale of Violence

ready for the harvest; the granaries, getting ready to be fed heavily.

One evening, Radha came with a big bowl full of meat steeped in garlic, cumin, and lemon and roasted on a raw coal fire. Mani kneaded wheat flour in jaggery syrup and fried small balls of that dough in mustard oil. The next evening, Mani and I took those sweet balls for Radha and her family. Always interested in gossip, the two women sat close to each other, eating the sweets with hot tea. Radha's sons ran across the house trying to hit each other.

'Donkey children, don't bother us,' harassed, Radha chided pausing her chatter for a second and resuming after ordering me to take the kids out. I took them to the balcony where they busied themselves in a 'hit and run game'. While they got busy playing, I looked out at the street changing its colour in the falling darkness. Suddenly, I saw Gurpal emerging from around the corner of the street. He was hurrying toward home. It was dark by that time, but streetlamps had lighted up. Street dogs rushed barking towards him. He hobbled up the stairs and as soon as he saw me, he shook his hand violently. He was too breathless to speak. He was telling me to come inside. I rushed to inform Mani about his arrival.

When we entered the house, we found him kneeling in front of Guru Nanak's picture hanging on the front wall. He was praying while moving his folded palms

MADAM MOHINI - A Romantic Tale of Violence

back and forth. What he spoke thereafter, was like a hodge-podge conversation. His face was tight and discoloured. The only thing I could make out was that he wanted the radio to be switched on. Mani was confused. I switched on the radio. It was time for the 8:00 pm news on All India Radio. The news of Indira Gandhi's assassination was the headline. The assailants were her Sikh bodyguards. Mani screamed with joy.

Mohinder rushed in at that moment. 'Riots... Riots...' he shouted. 'You are not safe here. The crowd that collected around the AIIMS roughed up the Sikhs in the vicinity. Even the president's car was stoned by the mob.' Panic tore his voice into pieces. He asked us to lock up our house and stay in his house till the time everything became normalised. And we did just that. News of rioting clouded the air and dark plumes of smoke cast a ghastly shadow over the sky. There was news of riots everywhere.

No one but Mohinder went out of the house and he always came back with news of the heinous crimes which were being committed unchecked by our 'powerful' state machinery. Mobs fanned out in many localities and looted Sikh-owned shops in shopping centres and local markets. There were some who were not directly involved in the action but they too stood in the form of crowds and watched the show, doing nothing. Such shows of live plunder and violence undoubtedly entertained them. You might wonder where was the

MADAM MOHINI - A Romantic Tale of Violence

police? To tell the truth, the police were also there, that too in large numbers and they too remained passive spectators of these live shows. Perhaps, they were asked by the government not to interrupt the 'show'. After looting, the shops were set on fire. Vehicles driven by Sikhs were also set alight. Soon this initial outburst of violence came under the expert guidance of well-known and well-connected leaders. They put their heads together and transformed this violence into a well-managed conflagration. Some of our worthy representatives in the parliament masterminded the whole situation. But it is easier said than done.'

A sarcastic grin erupted on Madam's lips. Sukhbir looked grim.

'First, they have to work at a psychological level and prepare the Hindus to riot. This is best done by floating rumours that Sikhs were killing Hindus. Rumours are highly potent entities, especially in our country. They travel at the speed of light and are immediately taken by the recipients as gospel truth The recipients then at once become vectors and transmit it to other recipients. Most of the time the vectors aim at transmitting it to more than one group of recipients. The number of vectors multiplies logarithmically. As the rumour passes through the vectors, it mutates either mildly or at times heavily. In case of a heavy mutation, the rumour of a minor scuffle between 'Ram and Sham' will result in Ram murdering Sham and then raping his sister. In

MADAM MOHINI - A Romantic Tale of Violence

case of a mild mutation, it would result in Ram hitting Sham on the head with a brickbat and Sham bleeding profusely."

Both of them laughed lightly at this graphic description of 'rumour'.

'So, after the psychological level comes the logistical level. For this, trucks were commissioned to bring in villagers from the outskirts of the city. These villagers were armed with iron rods and cans of gasoline. Then came the motivational level. The hired villagers needed an inducement to be violent. So, they were allowed to help themselves to whatever they could lay their hands on. Killing, arson, and rape were an additional bonus. Along with these incentives, they were also assured that the police will not interfere in their work. The rioters were also handed over the voter's list to help them locate Sikhs and their homes."

Madam fell quiet. Silence prevailed for some protracted minutes.

"Indira Gandhi had been assassinated on 31st October and so, the killings started in right earnest from the morning of November first and continued unabated till her funeral on the afternoon of November third. During this carnage, Sikh temples were burnt, Sikh men were brutally killed and Sikh women were gang-raped. Initially, the victims were bludgeoned with iron rods, then doused with petrol and set alight. In the later stages of the holocaust, a change was brought in the

✦ 64 ✦

MADAM MOHINI - A Romantic Tale of Violence

pattern of killings. They tied the victims' hands at the back and lowered burning tires around their necks. We were saved because Mani and Gurpal were not enrolled in the voter's list.

After two days of hiding, Gurpal went to the balcony to take a look at the situation outside. The air smelt like the air of a cremation ground. His eyes scanned the street. At the far end lay a charred three-wheeler. Feeble fumes of black smoke were still emanating from its amber body. A stray dog was cautiously sniffing it. After a few minutes of careful scrutiny, the dog started pulling out something.

Gurpal kept looking and what he saw a moment later shook him to the core. The dog pulled out a charred human body. A forceful retch cramped his gut and his stomach squeezed irresistibly. He threw up with a loud growl. A passer-by heard that and looked up. Gurpal walked in with shaking legs. His eyes and nose were watering. Mohinder had gone to the market to fetch some rice. I was helping Radha in the kitchen. Suddenly, we heard the main door squeaking open, and then it closed with a heavy bang. Radha and I rushed out of the kitchen. Mohinder, with unforeseen haste, was bolting the door.

'Don't keep looking at my face,' he turned and shouted at Radha. 'Go bring a lock.' Radha searched and brought it and Mohinder locked the door from inside.

'What happened?' she asked in a hushed voice.

+ 65 +

MADAM MOHINI - A Romantic Tale of Violence

'They know about Gurpal... somehow... I don't know how.' Panic-stricken Mohinder told Radha. Mani and Gurpal came into the room just then. Mani's legs were shaking with fear. I stood near the window and kept looking out at the thorny rose bush with my eyes riddled with pain. I stood unmoving, my hands by my side. Involuntarily, my hands rose to open the window. The breeze whistled in. I realised with a start that it carried a nasty stench — a stench of burning flesh and plastics. I felt a dull ache in my head. Radha coughed and rushed towards the window. She pushed me aside rudely and slammed the window closed.

Mohinder advised Gurpal to cut his hair but he was not ready for it. Radha made a sharp irritating sound. 'Don't be foolish. You will be killed.' He was finally brought around and a barber was summoned. While the barber's fingers were clicking rapidly Mani kept her gaze fixed on the floor. His hair fell in bunches and spattered the floor.

'Mani please...' Radha stood with a saree in her hands. 'Hurry up! Wear it.' Mani angrily brushed away her tears with the back of her hand.

'The truth is that we are hiding from ourselves only,' she murmured.

Hardly had the disguising procedure got over that we could hear slogans at a distance. The yelling became louder with every beat of my racing heart. The words became clearer as the shouting drew nearer.

MADAM MOHINI - A Romantic Tale of Violence

Khoon ka badla khoon se lenge.
Indira Gandhi zindabad.

And in no time, the horde was at the door.

'Hand over the Sardar,' one of them roared. I sprinted towards the kitchen and crouched behind the kitchen door, panting and sweating. Gurpal stood dumbfounded at one place. Every breath he took seemed penultimate. I heard voices and violent knocking at the door. With a trembling voice, Gurpal said, 'Don't open the door.'

Mohinder's hushed but forceful voice said, 'We will have to... Just pray to God.'

The door was opened. The slogans halted. Here and there, a cry shot up, 'Indira Gandhi *Zindabaad*'.

'Where is the Sardar?' A man croaked in a loud voice.

'There is no Sardar here, brother. You can search the house,' Mohinder gasped.

'Search,' the croaking voice ordered. I froze with fear.

'Who is this?' Asked the same voice, pointing at Gurpal.

'He is my cousin. He has come from my village,' Mohinder's voice was under perfect control. Some footsteps pounded near me. My knees squeezed together instinctively trying to keep themselves from trembling. A whimper escaped my lips.

'Aye girl, stand up,' a crude voice said over my head. I looked up. Two men stood looking at me. Their eyes were red and long red *tilaks* divided their foreheads into two grim portions. One of them, a haggard man,

+ 67 +

MADAM MOHINI - A Romantic Tale of Violence

bent over me and pulled me up with his rough fingers. My trembling legs found it hard to support my weight. He dragged me out of the kitchen. His fingers dug into my flesh but I could not feel any pain. I could not feel anything.

'Who is this girl?' the haggard man shouted while shaking me in his grip.

'My daughter, she is too scared.' Mohinder sounded muddled. It seemed everyone had forgotten about me and he was not prepared with an answer. The haggard man immediately released his grip. A man with a thirsty knife looked at saree-clad Mani from head to toe. Hastily applied vermillion flashed through her parting. The religious knife retreated into his cummerbund. The men armed with lathis, knives, and petrol left after satisfying themselves that there was no Sardar in the house.

Mani's face was hot and sweating. Gurpal was numb with fear. He burst out into a yell of pain. Tears ran down his freshly shaven face. Mohinder slapped his shoulders. A deep shuddering breath emitted out of Mani's lips and tears streamed out silently from her eyes too. I was too shocked to cry. I squinted out of the window through the dim light and found someone squinting back at me. He was dressed in spotless white and wore a Nehru cap on his head. He folded his palms and bowed with what seemed a permanent grin on his lips. Then he turned. He had another face at the back — dark as a ghost,

✦ 68 ✦

MADAM MOHINI - A Romantic Tale of Violence

blood dribbling out from his lips. With a little twitch of his features, he uttered – *Bharat Mata Ki Jai*.

As the minutes ticked away, the panic-ridden air started to ease. Then there was a knock at the door. Mohinder opened the door. Two men stared into his eyes. One was a dumpy man with a protruding belly and the other was the barber. Mohinder's breath stopped. The dumpy man elbowed the barber and he squealed at Gurpal. The man shouted, 'Come on, brothers.' And the horde returned. Colour evaporated from the faces of Gurpal and Mani. With folded hands, they asked for mercy. But for the mob, Gurpal had ceased to be a human being. The mob turned on to him like ferocious animals and beat him with rods till he dropped unconscious to the floor. Mohinder cried wildly urging them to leave him. But no one heard him. Radha had disappeared from the scene. Two men dragged Mani into the other room. She wriggled and tried to free herself from their grip. I stood there lifeless and stoned. Everything seemed unreal or I didn't want to believe that it was actually happening.

I wanted to close my eyes but was unable to do that as well. Mohinder turned to me and clutched me in his hug. He could not see that anymore. I was benumbed. I could barely move a muscle in my body. They rolled Gurpal in a blanket, doused it in petrol, and set it on fire. I saw him burning. I couldn't take my eyes off him. He was screaming. I saw his eyes through the red

MADAM MOHINI - A Romantic Tale of Violence

flame. After some infinite minutes, he fell quiet. The fire cracked. They dragged the burning coffin out of the room and left it on the balcony.

The dumpy man shouted at the men who were inside the room with Mani, 'Are you done?' And just then Mani's final blood-curdling scream was heard. I saw two men dragging Mani's half-naked blood-stained body out of the room. They took her body to the balcony and threw it over the burning coffin."

Madam was breathing heavily. Sukhbir felt alarmed, unable to believe what he was hearing. He quickly poured water into a glass and made her drink it. She looked at the edge of the window. She felt as if she was soaked to the lips in the stench and horror of that day. A strange disgust stole into her soul. A deep quivering breath escaped her mouth with a sibilant sound before she started narrating again.

"After a few hours, Mohinder sent me off to a refugee centre at Shayamlal College. An army contingent was managing the camp. But he promised to take me back as soon as possible. It's been so many years but I remember every little detail of that day. I tried hard to forget but I just could not.

Life at the camp brought more horrors. There were grieving people all around. The ones who got killed in the carnage were, in fact, fortunate. The numbers in the camp continued to swell daily. This resulted in lesser food and cramped spaces. For some days we were provided only bread and that too just once a day. But I was so consumed with shock that gnawing hunger ceased to pain me. I could not get the images out of my head. Along with that, I was also worried about how my mother would come to know where I was?

The stench of burning flesh oozed clammily from my every pore and every evening a headache tugged dully at my temples. I started suffering from nightmares, bolting awake in the middle of the night with my cheeks damp with tears. A poisonous, bewildering rage started building up inside me. Among the thousands of refugees, groaning, coughing, and snoring around me, I lay stiff under the tattered blanket which stunk of cockroach droppings. Gradually the number of refugees started reducing and the hall became quieter. Some of the people were taken home by their relatives, some by their friends, and some gathered the remains of their ruins and started their lives again. As the nights became leaner in people snoring and groaning in their sleep, my nightmares became more and more terrible. I started dreading the day when all but I would leave the camp.

The fields were bare, shorn bald of their crop. The dark underbelly of the soil got naked and was exposed to the winter sun. The land held the quiet of the afternoon in its palm, not a stray bark could be heard. There was not a person in sight. A kingfisher dived into the river and emerged triumphant a moment later with a tiny fish wriggling desperately in its beak. The hunter

MADAM MOHINI - A Romantic Tale of Violence

and the hunted made a natural order of things. And the shock, the bone-jarring jolt that I felt woke me up in the middle of the night. Only five people were sleeping around me, men and women, all old and all about to die. Hair raised on my back.

A fear often triggered hysterical bouts of crying. Mohinder had told me that he would come to take me but he didn't turn up. I sat huddled on the floor of the hall in a musty nook. The floor was cold and I hugged my knees to my chest. *Nothing worse could happen*, I told myself over and over. Acid rose in my throat and I swallowed hard. I began to rock back and forth, my arms wrapped tightly against myself. I saw red flames and a pair of burning eyes beyond the flames. I couldn't get the image out of my mind. I mechanically started hitting my head against the wall, once again, then again. I shut my eyes, willing myself away from the nightmares of the past few days, willing myself far from there, to the grass cushioning my feet, in my house in the village, to the smell of my mother's bosom and the chicken curry she cooked.

One hazy evening, when I sat watching the withering trees and pale grass of the lawn in front of the hall, I saw a man in uniform approaching me. He looked substantial. Another man behind him was trying to match his pace. They stopped near me.

'Do you have any relative?' the substantial one said in a stiff voice.

MADAM MOHINI - A Romantic Tale of Violence

I kept looking blankly at him.

'She doesn't speak, Sir,' the other one spoke in a low voice.

The substantial one knelt in front of me and repeated, 'Do you have any relatives?' this time he asked very softly.

I managed to shake my head. He prolonged his gaze at me and then looked away. 'We will have to send you to an orphanage.'

My expressionless face twitched and a sharp pain knifed through my body. I shrugged.

'Don't worry,' he kept his hand on my knee and craned his neck forward. 'They keep the children very nicely.'

I felt like a vulnerable animal. I pulled my knee from under his hand. He waited for a response but he didn't get one. And they left. The stench of burning plastics and flesh still stung my nose. I couldn't get rid of the smell. My heart was racing, my legs so weak that I could barely stand up. I was unable to sleep that night. I rubbed against the sheets for some relief. I kept my palms on my chest and stared deep into the dark ceiling. It seemed the ceiling exploded silently, crumbling into pieces that shot away into the space exposing the skies beyond it.

I watched the skies changing colour and the clouds changing shape. Substantial hollow clouds smothered the humble moon and the cheerfully blinking stars. I

✦ 73 ✦

MADAM MOHINI - A Romantic Tale of Violence

gasped horrified. The poisonous rage tore my nerves and I screamed as loud as I could. The few about-to-die people were startled out of their sleep. I pushed the blanket off me with a violent kick and leapt towards the door. I wanted to run out of that place. But the door was bolted. An old woman hobbled towards me. She groaned with every step she took. I rushed to the corner where a table was lying. I swept the bric-a-brac from the table and sent it crashing to the floor.

'Have you gone mad?' came the trembling voice of an old man. 'Have patience, child!' And he held me in his grip. I wrenched myself free from his grasp. I looked here and there with haunted eyes like a vulnerable animal.

That was one of the few fits of rage in my life which found expression. He caught hold of me again and stroked my head slowly a calm streamed into my body. My breath started easing and tears rolled out. 'You can't fight your destiny. All has been pre-written.' He looked into my eyes. His embalming voice pacified me further.

I can't pinpoint the exact time when I began thinking of it. But while piercing through the maddening grief the thought hit my mind that to succeed in this secular democracy one quality of character has to be deeply imbibed — be mean, but masquerade. Eat, if you don't want to be eaten up. I finally, calmed down.

One evening an army jawan reached out to me in overt sympathy nudging me awake as I dozed off near the wall in a long endless corridor. 'Aye, girl!' He spoke

MADAM MOHINI - A Romantic Tale of Violence

in a husky voice. I looked up at him hopelessly. 'There is someone to meet you.'

I nodded and waited tensely. An emotion surged up in my chest, so strong that I had to blink to stop the tears. I waited with my eyes shut. It would surely be my mummy. I assured myself. When I opened my eyes, I saw Mohinder coming towards me. His kindly eyes were clouded with concern as another man emerged from behind him — a young Sikh with a flowing beard.

Mohinder had written to Sikh families in Punjab regarding me. He had introduced me to each of them citing common acquaintances. He explained in every letter the urgency of his proposal. His letter read:

The girl comes from a good family and he personally vouches for her character. She is a girl with uncommon intelligence and a diligent spirit. It is clearly evident that she is ordained for larger things than being a mere occupant of an orphanage. She needs a mentor and you are the most suited for that. You have been chosen by the Gurus to have this opportunity. This one act of kindness will outweigh all the charities and pilgrimages you would do in your whole life. Help the girl with food and shelter if nothing more.

Response to one of his letters came one afternoon. He balanced the letter on his palm, gauging its heft, trying to judge from its weight the nature of the words within. Then soothing his long-awaited response on his lap, he began to finally read it with trepidation. His face

MADAM MOHINI - A Romantic Tale of Violence

remained impassive as he read through the letter. He re-read the letter twice and then carefully folded it and slipped it into an envelope. His younger son jumped into his lap. He absently stroked his hair as he sat lost in thought, pondering over his next step. The respondent wanted the girl as domestic help and to babysit his mentally challenged son. He was ready to take a pledge in the holy presence of the Guru Granth Sahib that he would provide good living conditions to the girl and keep her honour protected.

Only one response. There was no choice. And that is when the man came to take me with him. Once again, a wave of despair rose within me, so bleak, so abject that for an instant my vision seemed to blur.

'It was just... I wanted to...' Mohinder's eyes strayed towards that man, 'He has come to adopt you.' He finished calmly. He squatted in front of me. His eyes locked with mine in an intent searching gaze. I dropped my eyes.

'This is going to be good for you, child. He is a god-fearing gentleman.' He told me gently.

A shadow passed over my face.

'He is Gursimran Singh. He has a good house and a nice family. You will be happy there.' Mohinder told me quietly in a soft tone.

My lips quivered.

'And you know,' a smile appeared on his lips, 'he stays in Patiala.'

MADAM MOHINI - A Romantic Tale of Violence

An involuntary smile flashed across my lips and my eyes gleamed. I opened my mouth to express my acceptance but a sudden rush of excitement blanked my mind. I could not think of a word to say. All misery seemed to be extinguished at that moment. At last, I was going back to Patiala. There, my mother would be able to reach me easily. To everyone's surprise, I immediately got up to leave with that man.

'It would be dark soon and it is a long way to Patiala. You should leave,' Mohinder told Gursimran, who held my hand. I didn't even look at Mohinder as I left. But I felt his eyes at my back, watching me, unsure if he had made the right decision. I know he kept on looking at me till I was out of sight. He seemed relieved of a burden.

Soon I was in Gursimran's car. He was driving. The sun slipped further. Horns honked from all sides. The rage had left me with a rush, leaving me limp. I slept. It was quite dark by the time I woke up. I looked at the highway. The distance was fast being devoured by the car.

'What is your name?' Gursimran asked me lovingly.

'Mohanjit Kaur. Mohini.' I replied plainly without taking my eyes off the highway. Though I had travelled on this route only once I remembered everything. The moon sheathing every twig, branch, and leaf in silver, drawing pools of liquid shadow from under the parked trucks. The journey on that shimmering road was like

MADAM MOHINI - A Romantic Tale of Violence

a dream. A bat looped noiselessly through the air and then another. My eyes were dreamy. Doubt, despair, conviction, anticipation all had momentarily been laid to rest. I felt oddly light-headed.

We would be entering Punjab in an hour. It was 3:00 am and it was not safe to drive in Punjab before sunrise. So, we stopped at a *dhaba*, to eat and pass time. At 5:00 am we started again on our journey. As soon as we crossed the Haryana-Punjab border, darkness began to unravel. The night peeled away slowly as the sky flushed scarlet and shapes began to detach themselves from the mist. I took a deep breath. The sun began to push redly across the horizon and the sky was now pulsating with colours. Details began to reveal themselves. The moment passed as quickly as it had begun. The light faded as the sun receded into a dull glimmer far behind the clouds. The mist rolled back in, leaden and grey.

We reached Patiala around 8:00 am. The car stopped in front of a house in Model Town. Gursimran got out of his car and opened the main gate. The driveway was just enough for the car. A short and plump woman came out of the front door. They smiled casually at each other.

'How are you Pammi and how is Jeetu?' He asked the woman.

'Fine,' she answered coldly. They went in and I followed hesitatingly. Barely had Gursimran eased himself on to a chair that a boy bolted out of one of the rooms and dashed onto his lap. He kissed the boy and

MADAM MOHINI - A Romantic Tale of Violence

tickled his belly. The boy doubled up with laughter. The boy patted his face with his small hands, slightly smaller than mine. This was Gursimran's mentally challenged son Jeetu. Pammi poured water into a tumbler from a clay pot and offered it to Gursimran. Suddenly reminded of my presence, Gursimran said with a start, 'Look Jeetu, this girl will stay with us now.' Jeetu looked curiously at me. He did not seem interested in the introduction. A thought struck him and he pointed at his toys lying in one corner. He wanted to know if I would play with him or that was what I guessed he was trying to say. No one, neither Pammi nor Jeetu, was interested in knowing anything more about me, not even my name."

Madam's forehead frowned. She was pondering over something invisible. Her eyes were bright with tears. In all these years, Sukhbir had never seen her in tears. He could gauge the immensity of her pain.

* * * * * * *

Chapter 4

'In the beginning I just couldn't understand what was going on in that house. Pammi always flaunted around like a queen though she had nothing more than what even a queen's servant would own.' Madam opened her mouth in a feeble groan of agony. 'She would scold me whenever she saw me. She slapped me on my skull every time I made a mistake. She spent most of her day outside the house. I don't know what she did?

It was my second day in that house. I slept through the night lulled into an exhausting dreamless sleep. I was awakened by a sudden wild whoop of joy let out by Jeetu. Startled, I flung the blanket and rushed out of my room. He was nowhere to be seen. As I re-entered my room, he leapt on me from behind the door howling like a mad dog. My pupils dilated with fear. I peered at him and he pulled the most horrid face I had ever seen, squinting his eyes and protruding his tongue at me. I looked angrily at him and turned away. He spat disgustedly at my back. I slapped him on his cheek and

MADAM MOHINI - A Romantic Tale of Violence

he burst into wails. Sensing the trouble ahead I tried to quieten him.

'Ok, I am sorry. Please be quiet.' But he wouldn't listen. His screaming got louder and louder. I jumped to my feet and closed the door and scampered back to him. 'If you won't stop crying, I will not play with you,' I told him angrily. He got fascinated by the thought of play and abruptly fell quiet. I heaved a sigh of relief. 'You are a good boy,' I said instead what I wanted to say was, '*you retarded son of a bitch.*'

'What happened?' Pammi shouted from one of the rooms, putting on hold the phone on which she had been talking for what seemed like forever.

'Nothing, aunty,' I replied.

'Come here,' she screamed.

I looked at Jeetu with a jerk. I withheld the frown that was about to appear on my forehead and tried to smile at him, a fake smile was forced through my grim lips.

I went to her. She was still on the phone.

'Those days have gone. We can't wear sarees anymore,' she clucked remorsefully to someone on the phone. 'I looked so fabulous in a saree.' A smile appeared on her fat cheeks. She paused to listen. 'You are right!'

She paused again to listen.

'Thinking of buying a new salwar kameez,'

She paused once again to listen.

✦ 81 ✦

MADAM MOHINI - A Romantic Tale of Violence

'Silk, of course,'

She ignored my presence. I felt she hadn't noticed me and I turned to leave. But she snapped her fingers at me and gestured me to wait without stopping her conversation on the phone.

'Not only that, we have many other silk stores here. I always shop at Dwarka's though,'

Paused again.

'See you then. Bye,' and she kept the receiver at last. 'Hmm...,' and she wrapped her shawl tightly around her body and pulled herself out of the sofa in which she sat bundled. As she walked, the fragrance of a cheap jasmine perfume filled the room.

'Come, let me show you your work.' She breathed hoarsely as she moved her hand asking me to follow her. I walked behind her in the trail of her perfume. Jeetu had hidden behind the door and smiled at me. I didn't smile back.

Why didn't Mohinder tell me? I wondered. *He had painstakingly arranged a shelter for me. But when he did all that why did he then omit to prepare me for all this?*

The work started on the very second day. Cooking breakfast, lunch, and dinner, cleaning dishes, brooming and mopping the floor, washing clothes. I was supposed to do all that along with looking after that mentally retarded boy. He howled at the least provocation and threw tantrums like the son of a king.

✦ 82 ✦

MADAM MOHINI - A Romantic Tale of Violence

That evening he ordered me to play cricket with him. He always batted and never gave me a turn to bat. Tired after the day's work, I held the ball in a tight grip and let my rage uncoil into a crashing throw that straight away hit the wickets. And that was it. He swung the bat wildly in the air and roared insanely like a soldier shouting war cries. I took to my feet and ran as fast as I could. The day's exhaustion was forgotten and I just wanted to run away from that wild screaming animal. He was howling and running behind me.

Then it was quiet! I put a brake on my sprinting feet and turned. He was not there. I relaxed. I stood unsteadily on my trembling legs swaying from side to side. As soon as my heart slackened its pace, a lump rose up my throat, and tears rolled out of my eyes. At that very moment, a bat came crashing onto my head with such a force that I was propelled forward and fell with my face in the soil.

When I opened my eyes again, I was lying in bed. Gursimran was softly chiding Jeetu.

'Do you think you did the right thing?' Jeetu didn't look him in the eye. As I moved my hand, Gursimran looked at me with a relieved eye. He was sitting at the edge of my bed and Pammi was standing behind him.

'No hell has broken loose. The girl is alright,' she said with a haughty toss of her head. Jeetu would not look at them. He drew his knees up to his chin and gazed at the marbled floor.

MADAM MOHINI - A Romantic Tale of Violence

'Will you do it again?' Gursimran asked him pleadingly. Jeetu shook his head stoutly. Gursimran looked regretfully at me, patted my shoulder, and said, 'Take rest,' and left the room. Pammi followed him. Jeetu stayed on. He kept on gazing down and made a small sound in his throat, like a whimpering animal. Then he coiled himself and sat behind the door, peeping at me every now and then. When he looked at me, I made it a point to look away from him. Then he slowly crawled towards me. He looked up at me from the floor and smiled tremulously. I smiled back stiffly. He immediately let out a high-pitched whoop of joy. My hands instinctively rose to cover my ears.

My scalp ached. I kept on turning sides in the bed and waited for sleep to descend. I curled up under the quilt, squeezing my legs into my belly. It was the beginning of January. Winter was at its peak. It was a small room in the farthest corner of the house. A single bed by the tiny glass window and a three-legged stool was all that the room had. The bed was rickety and barely enough even for me. I looked out of the window of my room. All I could see were some wild bushes in the rectangular bed which ran along the foot of the boundary wall. One large irregular patch of plaster had come off the wall exposing the masonry behind it. A blanket of thick mist made the street lamp beyond the wall look translucent.

The smell of burning hair came back into my nostrils. Flames crackled over the corpse, wisps of smoke rising higher and higher. The flames were trying to enter all the nooks of his body, flickering over his belly and then a sizzling sound. His head exploded with a crunchy sound of a cheap Diwali cracker. I abruptly woke up from the nap, a scream trapped in my throat, just about to be released. My heart was hammering loudly. 'Mommy,' I mumbled and sobbed, burying my head in what could be called a pillow. The scene of Gurpal engulfed in fire kept playing over and over in my head. My head buzzed unbearably with the grief and horror which had metamorphosed into a sense of painful humiliation by then.

The air in the room got stuffy. I opened the window. A cold breeze wafted in through the open window. I shivered and my teeth chattered. The image of flames scorching his hair and the sound of sizzling flesh refused to leave me. I started shivering uncontrollably. I felt my scalp with my hand. The aching lump was still there. I pulled the quilt up to my nose. How I wished to run away from those memories! How I just wanted to get those images out of my mind.

If only I could get my mother back, my woes would end, I thought.

Some weeks passed and slowly I learned to live in that house. Jeetu never behaved better. Doing the household work was easier than handling him. He would hide in such places that probably, even ghosts could not discover. And if I couldn't find him, he would

MADAM MOHINI - A Romantic Tale of Violence

raise a hue and cry, every time the pitch was higher than the previous one. His mother would hear him and come screaming and shouting, 'Have we kept you here to make my son cry?' He would run to her and cry embedding his face in her spongy big belly.

I would hunt for him throughout the house, in the verandas, and bellow his name angrily but he never appeared. By then I knew most of his secret places — behind the wheat drum, under the bed, in between the bushes — but still failed to find him. Finally, I came to the junk piled up on the porch — smashed up iron containers, crumbled pieces of plastic, bottles of beer and whisky, and some stinking pieces of cardboard — to be later sold to the junk dealer. He sat huddled behind a discarded paint drum. My footsteps were as soft as feathers. I sat where I stood and stayed there, watching him. This was the right opportunity to snatch some moments of rest from all that running around which that moron made me do. After half an hour of complacent silence, he whimpered faintly in agony of the wait. But then again, he became quiet. At that moment, Pammi shouted, 'Oye Girl!... I am going shopping. I will return late.'

I kept quiet and didn't answer.

'Have you heard?' she shouted again. Then I heard her fashionable heels clicking away. She had left without waiting for my reply. It was a good chance. I stood up at once and squinted behind the drum. Jeetu jumped up and clapped with joy. I drew closer to him. My breath

MADAM MOHINI - A Romantic Tale of Violence

paced up. My lips tightened and my lower jaw moved as my lips gnashed together.

'You good for nothing, insane.' I spat and delivered a tight slap across his cheek. Ever ready to howl, he let out his cries as soon as he felt the impact.

'Cry louder.' My eyes flashed with anger. 'Let me see how loud you can cry.' He cried louder and louder. He didn't stop until his throat threatened to rip. After a long laborious session of howling, he finally stopped.

'If you tell your mother, I will kick you harder the next time,' I warned him sternly in a low yet firm voice. My finger wagged at him resolutely. I mouthed silent abuses on him until he walked away meekly and crept under his parents' bed where he stayed for the rest of the day. I had finally learnt how to deal with him which was the most important skill to imbibe to be able to survive in that house. He was a dumb boy. He could only utter some disjointed syllables from which his parents could barely make out what he wanted to convey. I decided to make sure that his syllables were reduced as far as it was possible. That was the first easy day I spent in that house.

Pammi returned in the evening, two bags of shopped goods hanging in her hands. She rolled inside. My heart dropped to my belly as soon as I saw her. *What if Jeetu tells her?* An apprehension scared me.

'Jeetu,' I called him aloud pretending to be playing hide and seek. 'Jeetu…' A soft call. Jeetu didn't reveal himself.

MADAM MOHINI - A Romantic Tale of Violence

'Dear Jeetu... Mommy... Mommy has come,' I said as politely as I could. He crawled out from under the bed.

'You were hiding here!' I acted perfectly surprised. 'I was looking everywhere for you. I sniffed grudgingly. He sat back on his haunches and looked at me like a frightened rabbit. He leapt behind Pammi and clung to her legs.

'What happened?' she tried to pull him from behind. My heart began to pound.

'Come on.' She pulled him but he refused to obey. 'Come on.' She was stern now. He reluctantly moved to the front. I crossed my fingers. *He will tell... Will he tell?* The thought kept buzzing in my head. He sobbed quietly but didn't utter a word.

'Aye girl, what is wrong with him?' she asked rudely.

'Nothing, aunty ji. A cat was sunning itself on the lawn. He reached forward to touch it and it snarled at him,' I quickly moved closer to him and put my arm around his shoulders, 'and he was frightened. Don't worry, Jeetu, it has gone now.' I said in a honeyed voice. He rubbed his ears and continued to sob.

'Alright.' She sat on her bed and ordered me to make some tea for her. Turning her head away, she fixed her gaze in the mirror on the front wall and started looking at her face from different angles. She hummed to herself in an unmelodious voice.

I knew the danger had passed. Jeetu stood still, glaring at me. I turned to go to the kitchen.

✦ 88 ✦

MADAM MOHINI - A Romantic Tale of Violence

That was my debut performance at pretensions. And I did perfectly well! It wasn't difficult at all. When Gursimran returned in the evening, he was surprised to see Jeetu so quiet.

'Why didn't you run to me, my son?' he tilted his head and asked. Jeetu continued squatting in the corner hurling his toys at the wall. He pushed his foot forward. Not uttering anything, he mutely propelled his foot further and pushed his toy car with a kick. Then he stood up and went away thumping his feet.

'The boy is testing my patience,' Pammi spoke from the bedroom and then walked out into the lobby where Gursimran stood. 'The whole day I run after this boy trying to keep him happy,' she said spitting out the orange seeds. I gave her a surprised look. She cringed a while and ignored me, 'but see, he always makes a face.'

'For goodness sake, stop grumbling. It is your duty,' he frowned at her while taking off his shoes.

'What do you mean? I don't do my duty!' she yelled furiously.

'Keep your voice low. Do you expect me to work all through the day at that wretched rice mill and then have the patience to listen to your ill-tempered babble in the evening?' he shook his hand vigorously at her.

Sensing the blackness of his mood she didn't retort and only shook her head in disgust and quickly left the room. He sighed inwardly, stretching his legs, and asked me to bring him some water.

MADAM MOHINI - A Romantic Tale of Violence

Days ticked away. The endless lonely nights and the nightmares showed no signs of leaving me. The days were the worst. Jeetu showed meek compliance for a few weeks after I slapped him which added some degree of comfort to my life. But this state of affairs did not continue for very long. Before I could realise, his behaviour started to change again. It all started one dull winter evening. I was sitting in the kitchen chopping the washed leaves of mustard to cook *saag*. It took me more than two hours to wash every leaf, arrange them in small bunches and then chop them. I heard voices from the room adjacent to the kitchen. Gursimran was talking to two men. The voices were diffused as the door of the room was closed. Whenever he needed something, his voice shot above the diffused voices, 'Aye girl...' I scorned this form of address. I had a name but no one called it.

'Aye girl, bring some water.'

I chopped faster. The clatter of the knife on the chopping board became louder and louder.

'Aye girl, didn't you hear,' he shouted. I banged the knife against the floor, stood up with a jerk, took out a bottle of water from the refrigerator, and thumped my feet towards his room. The two men wore white *kurta pyjamas* and blue turbans. Sword belts ran across their chests, half-covered by their flowing black beards. All of them were having drinks. One of them started, 'See, the matter is...' Gursimran faked a cough and flicked his

MADAM MOHINI - A Romantic Tale of Violence

eyes towards me. Abruptly, the man fell silent. I kept the bottle of water on the table and left. I could see Pammi sitting on her bed and applying nail polish to her witch-like nails.

I went into the kitchen and resumed my work. I put the chopped leaves into a big vessel and kept them on the stove to simmer at low heat. Since the kitchen slab was very high for me. Pammi had placed the stove on the floor. I started peeling garlic while stirring the leaves occasionally with a ladle. An aroma started emanating from the vessel, the most common aroma of our kitchens in winters. My mother used to cook the most delicious *saag*. She laboured for hours and mixed all the ingredients in just the perfect proportions and served it with *makki di roti*, butter, and ginger pickle. So lost was I in my thoughts that I didn't notice when Jeetu crept in soundlessly, stepping behind me. I continued working completely unaware of his presence as I mixed the peeled garlic in the *saag* simmering in the vessel. He stole up behind me and pounced with his characteristic wild whoop. I screamed in fright and glared at him in anger.

'Get lost,' I gritted my teeth. 'I have no patience for your foolish games,' I cried. I looked daggers at him. He pretended to cower. I resumed stirring the *saag*. He got enraged at my ignoring him and before I could judge his mood or react, he clasped my left arm tightly and dug his razor-sharp teeth into my flesh. My arm shook

MADAM MOHINI - A Romantic Tale of Violence

violently and the vessel full of hot and thick *saag* tipped. To my misfortune, the *saag* fell on his leg and feet. He started screaming at once. I stood dazed and frozen to the spot. My heart was rocking wildly.

'What happened?' Pammi came in shouting. As soon as she saw the *saag* on Jeetu's feet she too started screaming. Hearing her and the commotion, Gursimran rushed in. 'Oh! God,' he shouted. 'Take off his pants! What are you looking at?' He bellowed at me. I trembled. For the next two minutes, everything happened so fast and in the final second, I heard the car roaring away. They took Jeetu somewhere, perhaps to a doctor. I felt a twinge in my arm. I was reminded of the bite. His front teeth had pierced my flesh and it was bleeding painfully. My eyes filled with tears and I looked unhappily into space.

I sat mutely near the main door like a dog waiting for its master. A dog and a servant are expected to behave alike. I didn't really realise when I became a servant and when I actually submitted. My head was buzzing, my heart beating as if it might explode and yet I was filled with stillness. This is how a servant should stay. A fear deadweighted in my heart. With every passing minute, the fear loomed larger. The chilled wind of that winter night did not make me shiver. I stayed there, near the door, squatting on the cold floor.

After two hours they came back. Jeetu clung around Pammi's chest as she hobbled in. His feet were

MADAM MOHINI - A Romantic Tale of Violence

bandaged. My eyes crossed Gursimran's eyes. They were red. A heartbeat later, he swirled around the corner and slapped me on my right cheek. Before I could feel the pain of the first, a second came crashing onto the left cheek, then another, then another, then a push. I fell down on the floor. Then he drew back his leg and kicked with such a force that I buried my teeth in my lip to keep from crying aloud. I felt the salty taste of blood in my mouth. I was bleeding. He gasped. I raised my head slightly. Pammi stood there. She was smirking.

Bruises were slowly blossoming on my skin where ever he had kicked. Beneath them, a poisonous bitterness began to flourish and spread in my body. I barely made it to the washroom and vomited. I continued to retch into the sink long after my stomach was empty. Anger flared up inside me —the impotent anger of a servant. I went and lay down in my bed. I flipped sides under the quilt. Every side ached. Every inch of my body ached. Humiliation crept over my skin like worms. I was split into three parts, left, right, and I, which talked and argued the whole night.

I: I will not let this go unavenged.

Right: But You can't avenge it.

I: I will.

Right: You are just a little helpless girl how will you avenge it?

Left: Why don't you run away?

MADAM MOHINI - A Romantic Tale of Violence

I: But where can I go?

Left: You do have a house in your village. You can go there.

I: But no one is there.

Left: And who is here?

I: But how will I sustain myself?

Left: Come on. You know how to do household work. You can work in people's houses. You will be able to earn enough to sustain yourself. Leave these thankless people.

I: You are right. My mommy can also find me there.

Right: Stay here. You won't be safe there.

I: Yes, I won't be safe there.

Right: Moreover, you can avenge a person only by staying with him.

Left: Don't be afraid. A coward dies many times before his death. Go and embrace freedom. Freedom brings responsibility. You have to be prepared to handle responsibility.

I: Yes, I have to be free.

Left: Moreover, you can search for your mother. Staying here will not help in looking for her.

I: Yes, you are right.

The next morning, I started the routine work more carefully than normal and tried to look as busy as possible. Gursimran left for work. As soon as he left, Pammi garbed herself in a gaudy dress and clicked away,

MADAM MOHINI - A Romantic Tale of Violence

but not before giving me detailed instructions about lunch, dinner and other works. The special instructions were regarding Jeetu's medicines.

A plan was ready in my mind. All I had to do was wait for the junk dealer. I warmed a cup of milk for Jeetu, added my spit and sugar to it, stirred it, and gave it to him. He was not looking very happy that morning. I went outside and blinked in the sudden sunlight. I paced up and down the veranda, waiting anxiously for the junk dealer. The day was bright, the sky spotlessly blue. The pain of yesterday's thrashing popped up as and when my mind paused from thinking about the plan. I sat against the wall. The solidity of the bricks behind me was strangely comforting. It was around 11:00 am that I heard the distant voice of the junk dealer.

'Sell old books, newspapers, bottles, iron scrap...' he was bellowing.

I rushed to the porch and started taking out the junk. The dealer was coming nearer. In five minutes he was at the door. He weighed the stuff and gave me thirty rupees.

'Thirty rupees!' My eyes grew big with excitement. I could not believe that I had thirty rupees in my hand! I jumped up and down with joy. I hastily brought my bag which contained my house's key, a dress, and my doll. Then I took a deep slow breath, willing myself to calm down. I took a firm and fearless step forward and walked briskly out of that house into the street. It

MADAM MOHINI - A Romantic Tale of Violence

seemed like I was floating on my buoyant feet. I rushed onto the road. Scooters, cars, cycles, and rickshaws were happily drifting by. I took a rickshaw to the main bus stand. The air was winding around me dreamily. From the bus stand, I took a Rajpura bound bus that would stop at Kauli.

I alighted from the bus and stepped onto the soil of my village. A strange unidentified feeling crept up. Was that fear? Yes, now I know it was fear. Freedom is actually frightening, especially when one has submitted to servitude. Slowly, though, I began to notice the hush around. My eyes were drinking in the beauty of the rutted road which led to my house. I thumped my feet. Fine dust rose up. It smelt like nectar to me. I started walking towards my house. I willed myself to compact the awful memories of the past years and start living anew. At last, I was back. A vague hope sprang up in some corner of my heart. The hope kept growing with every step I took, the hope that my mommy will open the door for me.

My steps paced up. I started moving faster though I kept my gaze fixed on the ground. My bag swung merrily around my neck. As I reached the front of my house, I took a deep breath and mustered the courage to look up at the door. It was locked. Other than one small corner, the rest of my heart knew. A dull pain crossed that corner. Tangles of thorny bushes had erupted around the main gate. Wild grass had grown knee-deep.

MADAM MOHINI - A Romantic Tale of Violence

I opened the iron gate of my home and waded my way through the grass up to the front door.

I opened the lock and pushed the door. It was jammed. I pushed harder and it opened with a hoarse squeak. A stale stench like that of moth-eaten loads of files cramped up in an archive, wafted out. Every object in the house was covered with a thick layer of dust. Vast, elaborately spun cobwebs bridged the gap between the things. Fungus had created a grey velvet patchwork on the front wall. Yet, the house was simmering with dangerous compelling beauty. I looked around with a pang of sorrow, sadness engulfing me. The house was moaning.

No one has come here since you left.

My chest felt knotted. I was close to tears. But I knew instinctively what I had to do now. The first thing was to clean up. I grabbed the broom. Its straws were brittle but good enough to serve the purpose. I took an old rag and focused all my energy on cleaning the house, one of the skills I had learnt in my servitude.

By evening I was hungry. I went to the corner shop to fetch some bread. The shopkeeper looked at me with surprise. 'Where have you been?' he asked in a mysterious voice. I kept quiet for a while, 'Give me some bread,' I said giving him three rupees.

'Where are your parents?' he asked while handing over the bread to me.

'I don't know,' I replied and walked away.

MADAM MOHINI - A Romantic Tale of Violence

I ate some slices of bread with water and kept the remaining for the days to come. I could clean the kitchen and drawing room by night. I lay on the *Diwan*, dead tired. The moments seemed to be simply passing. Nothing else could be done till morning when I had decided that I would get up and go out in search of work.

In the morning. I went to the house next door. The lady of the house came out. I remembered her face.

'What?' she asked without wasting time.

'Aunty ji, may I work in your house?' I asked her politely.

'Work? For free?' She questioned.

I shook my head.

'I don't have spare money. Moreover, my bones are intact. I can work myself,' she was unreasonably angry.

I then thought of going to some big house that could shell out some money for domestic help. So, I walked to the Sarpanch's house. The big gate was open. I had just gone a few steps when a jeep entered behind me. The Sarpanch was driving it. He stopped by me and came out.

'Aren't you Kartar's daughter?' He asked curiously.

'Yes,' my face brightened up.

'Where is Kartar?' he creased his forehead.

'I don't know,' I sighed.

'What are you here for?' he asked plainly.

'If you can give me some work, I will serve you with my soul,' I folded my hands and pleaded.

MADAM MOHINI - A Romantic Tale of Violence

He smiled and patted my head, 'Come with me.'

I blinked my eyes in surprise. They were beaming. I was amazed at how simple it was. *I was unnecessarily languishing at Gursimran's house*, I thought. I walked behind him with a spring in my feet and hope in my heart. He sat on the string cot lying in the vast courtyard, under a huge mulberry tree. He made me sit beside him.

'Pappu's ma...' He called aloud for his wife. I sat calmly devoid of apprehensions and fears. I watched a servant putting fodder in the manger for the buffaloes. There were six of them — black and shiny with curled horns. Another servant came with buttermilk in a brass tumbler.

'Oye, bring for this girl, too,' the Sarpanch ordered.

My stomach rumbled at the thought of buttermilk and I realised I was hungry. The servant turned and went back into the house. The Sarpanch started gulping down the buttermilk. I looked at him and my mouth watered. He cleaned the drops of buttermilk that clung to his moustache and kept the tumbler down. I shifted my gaze in the direction from which the servant would come with the buttermilk and saw him emerging from around the corner. He could have walked faster. I stood up and marched towards him. I took the tumbler from him and swallowed the contents greedily. My stomach was pacified. I went back to the cot and sat down. The Sarpanch looked at me and smiled. Bibi, the Sarpanch's wife, reached there the next moment. She adjusted her

MADAM MOHINI - A Romantic Tale of Violence

dupatta on her head and said, 'Yes.' Then she looked at me and asked, 'Who is she?'

'That Kartara, you remember?' The Sarpanch tried to scratch her memory.

'Oh! Kartara?' she exclaimed in a low voice.

'She is his daughter and she wants some work at our house.' He told her in a soft tone.

'I heard he is wanted, so is his wife.' She looked curiously at me. A buffalo shook her head to ward off the flies and the bell around her neck clinked.

'That is right but how does it matter?' The Sarpanch looked casually at her.

'Have you gone mad? Come with me,' and she took him aside. My heart dropped and my cheeks went hot and red. A gust of wind brought the smell of buffalo dung and urine. After five minutes, the Sarpanch returned. He shook his head regretfully at me. I nodded, my eyes brimming with tears. He looked crestfallen as the tears started running down my cheeks. I turned to go back.

'I will send food for you,' he said. I kept walking.

I begged people, even went down on my knees. But no one gave me work. Everyone pushed me away. Initially, I cried and cried. But gradually, tears refused to come out. Then I pretended to cry by pulling the most miserable face one could ever imagine. But nothing worked. Some rejected me because my parents were wanted and others rejected me for fear of getting polluted by my touch.

MADAM MOHINI - A Romantic Tale of Violence

My persistence slowly started bothering the villagers. They instructed their children to keep away from me. As soon as I attempted to join a group, it melted away. When I tried to speak with someone, they behaved as if they were deaf. Slowly, a feeling of hatred for everyone started fermenting into a fury within me. My heart plunged deep into despair. The fury became stronger and bigger with each passing day.

Ten days had passed. There was no breakthrough. Neither had I got any clues about my mommy, nor had I got any work. The Sarpanch's servant came every evening with four chapattis, mango pickle, and a tumbler of buttermilk. I would eat two chapattis for dinner and save two for the morning. The Sarpanch's courtesy made me go on till the fury grew monstrous. I cried aloud that night. Streams of frustrated tears kept gushing out for almost an hour. The monster of that fury belittled the feelings of vengeance I had for Gursimran.

I thought of going back.

The next morning, I stood at Gursimran's door. He was wiping the dust off his scooter and was ready to go to work. Jeetu was watching him doing that while his hands were busy playing with his toy car. They both noticed me at the same instant. All movements of their limbs paused. Some emotions crossed Gursimran's face in quick succession. First and quite recognizable was that of anger. The others which followed were

MADAM MOHINI - A Romantic Tale of Violence

unrecognizable and perplexing. I cast my eyes down to avoid looking confused. He walked up to me. I tightened the flesh on my bones to reduce the impact of an imminent blow from him. But contrary to my apprehensions, he curled his arm around my shoulders and said politely, 'This is your own home. Never do it again. Never run away from here.' I looked up at his face. He smiled.

Jeetu thumped his feet on the floor to emphasise disgust and ran inside.

'See how happy he is,' Gursimran said looking at Jeetu.

I gave a half-smile for I knew that Jeetu was not happy to see me.

'Can you handle the boy for some time? You people have made my life miserable,' Pammi shouted from inside. The next moment she appeared at the door dragging Jeetu in her firm grip. She looked ruined. Her untidy hair and flour-stained hands made her look devastated. As soon as her eyes fell on me, she beamed in a way I had never seen before. She released her grip on Jeetu and he fell with a thud.

'Thank god...thank God,' she uttered loudly. She was unable to manage the expression of joy on her face. No one could ever be so happy on seeing me. In a way, I felt obliged and my heart warmed towards her.'

* * * * * * *

Chapter 5

Sukhbir had a lean face with a fuzzy aureole of black beard obscuring every part of his face under his nose and cheekbones. He liked to think that his beard was functionally important. He was a tall and active man of paralysing stupidity and full of uncalled-for enthusiasm. It was only his unquestioning loyalty to her that made him indispensable to Madam. He was one of the devoted drudges whom she could depend upon.

Sukhbir's hands were joined at his back. Madam looked disinterestedly around the room. Her eyes paused for a moment at the framed portrait of Guru Nanak in a yellow robe, hanging on the wall she was facing. The Guru carried a solemn benevolent smile on his face and his open hand forever sent indiscriminate blessings to all. Madam resorted to quieter deliberations.

* * * * * * *

'We have such indiscriminate looking Gods in India but often it is their indiscrimination itself which results in

MADAM MOHINI - A Romantic Tale of Violence

a lot of discrimination. This discrimination is made to look divinely ordained whereby it acquires an element of self-sustainability. And the person who suffers from such discrimination becomes mentally conditioned to blame God for all his woes which could be his unemployment and starving family, the uncovered and overflowing drain in front of his house; or no power supply for almost eight months a year. The common opinion about God among these people is that He gives to those who already have and not to those who don't. God's undesirable behaviour is then attributed to *kalyuga*, which becomes the explanation for the unexpected.'

'But then they conveniently also forget that the ones who 'have', give a lot to the Gods in return,' Sukhbir added from his practical 'wisdom'.

'You are right, Sukhbir. They celebrate the 100, 200, 300, 500 years, and so on of Gods' births and other important events of their lives, that too on a grand scale with a lot of pomp and show. They preside over huge religious ceremonies and inspire the common man to revere the gods and be happy in whatever condition he keeps them. Now look at our Chief Minister, he renders tremendous service to the gods. He has a brave and devout heart to spend crores of rupees on such celebrations. And people also acknowledge his services. They vote for him again and again, though intermittent remonstrations do occur at times. But the people of Punjab are extremely wise as they know that *service to*

✦ 104 ✦

God is service to mankind. When you serve God in a big way, he also rewards you in a big way. The rewarded ones then buy the services of the unrewarded ones with a promise to ameliorate their lot from drudgery. But it is not their fault if they almost always fail to deliver. They fail because they are not ordered by the Gods to deliver. So, finally, it is the Gods who have to be brought to book and not the ones who 'have'.'

Madam smiled at Sukhbir and he smiled back in resonance. She roused herself from her seat at the window and sat up straighter. She let out a belch and sat back again, slightly proud of her power. She slipped her hand under her bun and rubbed her neck as though it had stiffened. Her face was completely inscrutable. She had acquired this expressionlessness with a long and conscious effort. This was required because there were some eyes that were always watching her. You might not be able to see them but they were there, like ghosts — someone might always be eavesdropping. Asleep or awake, working or bathing, indoors or outdoors, there was no escaping them. Not even a week passed that some sting operation or the other made it to the headlines. Scams and scandals involving either sex or money were their favourite topics of investigation. One could conceal things only with a consistent and unfaltering composure. One has to learn how to dodge successfully and continue doing so forever. And, she had become an expert at it.

She looked up at the ceiling and closed her eyes, going back in time. The trembling movement of her eyeballs under her eyelids failed her efforts to hide the restlessness. She started understanding the feeling of helplessness, futility and emptiness of it all. She seemed uncertain as to why she had done all that? Had she done it for the past, which had ceased to exist except in some centimetres of her brain — those centimetres which sometimes inflated to belittle the rest of her brain and sometimes squeezed painfully to a heavily compacted dot? But that dot pricked her memory like a pin. Or, had she done it for the future, which had always been uncertain and would continue to remain so? A tremendous uproar of thoughts continued within her brain.

She could not remember a time when she was not at war with her situation but it was also true that there had been a long interval of peace during her childhood. Then an image flashed — people sitting on the floor, she too was sitting there among them. An old man and a woman were sitting near her. The old man wore a white suit and a hurriedly wrapped turban on his head. His face was red and his deep eyes were full of tears. She felt the pain of unbearable grief oozing out of his eyes. She knew that something terrible, something which was beyond forgiveness had happened to him too. The horrors of the refugee camp post riots never stopped pricking her. Then she saw her mother flying away

MADAM MOHINI - A Romantic Tale of Violence

and disappearing. She saw a flash of knowledge in her mother's face, the knowledge that she might go so that her daughter could live. Her mother's memory tore at her heart. She disappeared loving her.

An ear-splitting roar of a fighter jet passing overhead through the sky startled her. She sprang out of her memory. Momentarily she caught Sukhbir's eye. He had taken off his spectacles and was in the act of resettling them on his nose with his characteristic gesture. There was that fraction of a second when their eyes met. Sukhbir gave her an ever-pleased smile.

He had often been surprised by her decisiveness and deep political wisdom. She would deliberate for some minutes and then speak out in a casual tone, even the most important decisions. At times, she wouldn't even speak. Not a line on her face would move. Just her motionless eyes would shoot a sharp glare or a gesture or two would convey the message. That's it. And Sukhbir almost always understood. As it happened one summer day when the sun was so hot that it could melt the tar on the roads and heat the earth till it burnt under the feet. The air in the room was tense. Madam was looking at the morning sky through the window. She was watching an eagle being chased away by a flock of crows.

'Are you sure he has valid documentary evidence?' she had asked without taking her eyes off the eagle.

'Yes, Madam. I checked them myself,' Sukhbir sounded worried. 'He also has some audio recordings.'

MADAM MOHINI - A Romantic Tale of Violence

'Very good!' she turned with a jerk and glared at him. 'This habit of yours is making me mad,' she looked very angry. 'Why can't you stop giving the most important information in a way of the least important one?'

'Sorry, Madam,' he stood up.

'I guess next you will tell me that he has a video recording too!' she said sarcastically.

A silence followed her statement. Madam breathed deeply. Sukhbir stood with his head hung to his chest. The aerial view of his head could be seen from the front. His blue turban looked like a boat with his round bun of hair popping at its centre.

'Shall we talk to the owner of this channel? Perhaps, the owner can persuade him to reach a deal with us or fire him,' said Sukhbir, hesitatingly.

'If he doesn't agree we will unnecessarily have a new mouth to feed. And in case he is fired, the problem will stay as he would then be able to sell his findings to some other channel or newspaper. There are countless of them these days,' she said thoughtfully. 'Offer him Rupees one hundred thousand.'

'I did but...' Sukhbir started answering.

Madam cut him short and unfolded her strategy, 'First, we will secure ourselves. His actions are only for money, but our reputation is also at stake. I can't risk my ticket for the next assembly,' she rubbed her hands and sat down abruptly in the chair. The turbulence of her mind could be seen on her face. A muscle

✦ 108 ✦

twitched in her face. She picked up the tiny statue of Buddha lying on the table and turned it upside down. She twirled it on its head for some moments, deep in thought. Sukhbir waited impatiently for her to say something. He shifted his weight from one foot to another.

She started speaking in a slow and deliberate whisper. Sukhbir leaned forward to hear. She looked up sternly at his face and he moved back at once, like a spring. Then she took out a toothpick from one of the drawers of her desk, held it with both hands at its tips as if gauging its strength. She looked intently into Sukhbir's eyes. The skin on the sides of her eyes creased a little. The sharpness of her gaze was decisive and Sukhbir knew that the discussion was over. She broke the toothpick. It made a woeful cracking sound.

'Yes, Madam,' Sukhbir said.

There had been a business-like understanding between them which was exactly required. He had all that was required to be a politician's PA — meanness, shrewdness, and orthodoxy to be conscious of the truth while being able to perfectly tell carefully constructed lies. A task assigned to him was a task done, especially when it concerned eliminations and disappearances. He had an appreciable understanding with the police and the *gundas*. The unwanted people would simply disappear especially during the night. Instantly, a warm wave of relief flowed through her. Once again, she

MADAM MOHINI - A Romantic Tale of Violence

glanced at the sky and thought, *the destruction of truth was a beautiful thing.*

* * * * * * *

The sun was setting. She sat with her eyes focused on a blank space. She was conscious of nothing but the blank space in front of her. The interminable restless monologue that had been running inside her for years could not stop asserting itself. She felt a twinge of pain in her chest. She thought about what Sukhbir might be thinking. He might want to go. But the eagerness of his waiting eyes conveyed to her that he wanted to listen to the story further. He wanted to know everything that she had to tell.

'It was always early morning and it was still dark when I was shaken out of my dreams,' she uttered quietly. 'A villainous cheap scent of some cheap *agarbatti* hung in the morning air. I would drag my feet to the kitchen, sleep still crouching in the corners of my eyes and prepare tea for Gursimran and his wife. Through the kitchen door, I would see him sitting cross-legged on the bed with a little book. Every morning, he recited hymns from it. The continuous stream of sound which poured out of his mouth sounded like the quacking of a duck. It was impossible to distinguish even one word from another. Some words were jerked out rapidly which sounded distinct from the rest of it which was mostly noise. Yet

MADAM MOHINI - A Romantic Tale of Violence

there was no doubt about the general nature of those recitations — it was all about the glory of God. But I always had a curious feeling that it was not his heart or mind but only his throat which recited the hymns. He uttered with the zeal of venomous orthodoxy. His little eyes never stopped darting suspicious glances from side to side during the whole process. Irritated at his quack-quack, I would try to take my ears to distant sounds. But those were also an annoying mix of numerous such sounds coming out of innumerable gurudwaras and temples.

Pammi would scuttle nimbly through the corridors entering one room leaving another. Her short legs kept growing stouter with each passing year. She seemed to be the only one who flourished in that house. Every day, she would apply face packs each of a different material — sandal, turmeric, or basil. But nothing could stop the deepening of the creases on her face. While doing her morning routine, she would keep looking at me in a sidelong way, watching the expressions on my face.

I always had an overwhelming temptation to shout filthy words at her at the top of my voice or bang her head against the wall to take out my frustration which was building up day after day after day. But I could never do any of those things. I could never let my frustrations of being a servant manifest themselves. I could not even repent my coming back to that house

MADAM MOHINI - A Romantic Tale of Violence

simply because I had no other choice. How could I think of an alternative since there was none left? The best way for me was to stop thinking and be like an animal — eating, working, and shitting. I had decided to train my mind into not thinking and not feeling and to continue working mechanically. It seemed merely a question of self-discipline and reality control. But it was not so easy to accomplish.

Things in that house were changing fast. Now, more and more men started visiting Gursimran and he always held closed-door talks with them. Within a year of my return, he had left his job and had started devoting his evenings to entertaining his guests. I was also kept on my toes serving the guests. In the beginning, they would stay only for an hour or so but this gradually expanded to fill the whole evening till late at night. One of them was a fat middle-sized man called 'Billa'. He might have been in his early thirties but he had already accumulated layers of fat around his waist and belly. They danced when he walked and more so when he laughed. One could never hear him laughing, only see. He would let out quick forceful bursts of air accompanied by low hissing sounds from his lungs. Only by looking at his animated body could you find that he was laughing — a jumping belly, a quivering huge beard, mouth open wide to show all his teeth and watering eyes. His movements were brisk and boyish. He looked like a boy who had grown large. He was always dressed in a shirt

MADAM MOHINI - A Romantic Tale of Violence

and pants. The shirt remained neatly tucked in his pants until he was some drinks high. Neat folds of his turban, which was mostly blue, continued providing him with the look of a gentleman, even when he became shabby below his head.

He greeted everyone cheerfully, even me when he entered the home. He would pat my head and smile at me and I would smile back. That was the only moment in a day when I smiled. I waited for that moment. It was curious how often I thought about him. For some reason, his smile suddenly made me think and feel the faculty I was trying to suppress. His smile was failing my effort but I liked that failure. It was relieving. It made me think of freedom, which was as unimaginable at that time, as a fish flying in the sky. I found myself happy doing services when he was there. I served soda water and ice cubes when they were having drinks and prepared snacks and salads for them. I tried to make maximum trips to the room where they sat and tried to stay there as long as possible. At times, this irritated Gursimran and he would say harshly, 'Go now, don't linger.'

At this Billa almost always had a polite intervention, 'Come on, let her. She is just a little girl'. And he would smile again at me. That is when Gursimran started instructing in the day and strictly told me to be nimble at work and stay for the minimum possible time around the guests. But when Billa was there, I would nerve myself to break the rules and disobey him.

MADAM MOHINI - A Romantic Tale of Violence

I don't remember why I wanted to do that. Was it a child's curiosity to hear what they talked or was it to see Billa's bright smile and his mute laughter? He was unlike the others who visited that house. I was fascinated by him. I could feel that the degree of his orthodox fanaticism was somewhat lower than that of the other guests who came to the house. Though he venerated Bhindranwale, he rejoiced over the assassinations performed by young terrorists, he sincerely hated Hindus, yet there was something subtly different about him. It was clear from his clothes and behaviour that he was a very rich man. Perhaps this was the reason for Gursimran's hospitality. Billa would say things that would have been better left unsaid. He talked about his associates, the young militants who had carried out many courageous killings and assassinations. He even talked about their future plans, well within the range of my hearing. I heard him talking about the guns and where they were hidden? Where to get new ones from? And where and with whom the money was parked?

He talked fearlessly about everything and smiled at me when I pretended to be busy with some work in that room. Gursimran felt restless with my presence. His small eyes flittered nervously from me to Billa and from Billa to me, but Billa could never take a cue and shut his mouth. Gursimran's helplessness reflected his dependence on Billa for some earned and expected benefits. But his helplessness filled me with an

MADAM MOHINI - A Romantic Tale of Violence

inexplicable sense of satisfaction. Once, a scream of joy rose so forcefully up my throat that I had a hard time trying to quell it. It still escaped in the form of a feeble whimper. I enjoyed those moments in that room, spiced up by the smell of liquor mixed with the smell of fish or chicken. I was too young to keep my features perfectly under control. It is possible that Gursimran could read that look of subconscious joy on my face. As a result, within a week my evening schedule was altered. I was shifted out of the kitchen to stay around Jeetu and the reigns of all hospitality were taken over by Pammi.

No one could ever guess how her hospitality would change things. Everyone, including me, underestimated her potential. More men started giving Gursimran and his wife the pleasure of their company. Some of them would stay till late at night and some even till morning. But there were some who did crisp business only. They exchanged some information, money, and arms and left as briskly as they had entered. These men were slightly more obsessed with the mission than the rest of them.

One night, like every other night, I sat alone in my room after making Jeetu go to sleep. Gursimran was busy doing some calculations on paper. He held an ink pencil in his hand and wrote while Billa was dictating some figures. I tiptoed out of my room not out of pure curiosity. Surely, something else was also behind this act of mine which I didn't know at that time. Perhaps, it was a desire to see Billa or maybe just to know from

✦ 115 ✦

MADAM MOHINI - A Romantic Tale of Violence

what I was being barred. I don't know the reason but I stepped out of my room and peeped through the slight opening between the door curtains.

I remember the terrified fascination with which I watched them. The glamour of an underground struggle and the risky mission was sticking in the air around them. There was another person in the room. I had seen him before also. His name was Sukkha. He was not a regular visitor. He always carried an expression of haste on his face. His brisk hand movements showed that his hands were full with assignments. His small face looked smaller under the weight of a huge untidy turban. Only a small part of his cheeks was beard free. The suppleness of his cheeks made me guess that he might be in his twenties. His small eyes flashed rebellion. His beard covered his neck and tapered to an end just below it. His face was flushed. He was sitting very straight in his chair; his weak chest inflating and deflating with a force.

'With this much, we can buy only two guns. We urgently need four,' he spoke with a sort of Pedant's passion.

'I said the same to Billa Sahib,' Gursimran said with fake enthusiasm.

'Alright,' he drank something from a mug, perhaps tea, and continued speaking, 'I have asked for it. We will manage. But...'

Billa interrupted him, '...you continue with your talk. I will be back shortly,' he said while standing up. He

MADAM MOHINI - A Romantic Tale of Violence

looked at Gursimran and their eyes met for a second. Their glances communicated a sort of understanding that I was unable to comprehend.

I ran back to my room as soon as I saw Billa coming out of the room. I watched him. He went to Gursimran's bedroom and closed the door behind him. I kept on watching. He came out of the room after ten minutes, adjusting his turban. This time he did see me. He smiled in his characteristic way. But I didn't smile back. I looked into his eyes. He cast his eyes down. I am not fully certain why I did all that? He crossed the lobby in quick steps. He stopped for a second before entering the room where Gursimran sat. I thought he would turn back and tell me to mind my own business and remind me of my servanthood. But he did nothing of the sort and went inside. My teeth were on edge. I wanted to spit. I reminded myself that I was not to think or feel. But it didn't work. The urge to shout filthy words at Pammi had emerged even stronger. What I was feeling was curiously inexplicable. I was feeling cheated!

My attention drifted back to the room where they all sat. Something in Sukkha's face suggested irresistibly that he would be eliminated. In that group of revolutionaries and so-called revolutionaries, some would perish and they would leave the ones who cleverly survived, richer — politically as well as economically. In my mind's eye, I had a vision of Punjab, vast and ruinous, with large tracts of barren

✦ 117 ✦

MADAM MOHINI - A Romantic Tale of Violence

land where millions were slogging through dreary jobs, wearing worn out and dirty clothes. And at the same time, there were some, who would be living in the castles guarded by the state police, trying to manage tons of currency notes by packing them in gunny sacks, stacking them in their basements, or parking them hideously in foreign banks.

Their heads in blue turbans would rule the unquestioning millions through the Gurudwaras. The religious coefficient of politics would be kept high to fool the people. A durable feeling of primitive patriotism would make people accept what would otherwise be unacceptable. Whether the revolution succeeded or failed, Punjab could not be saved. Like iron is eaten up by its own rust, the ones who would survive would eat up Punjab. When democracy is followed in a letter it brings no big surprises or shocks to its leaders. It is only when the spirit of democracy is touched that the chairs begin to shake and tumble. So the spirit has to be carefully left to sleep.

My learning had started.

I could not formulate exactly where our lives were going. With their glittering and terrifying guns, they were a bunch of warriors and fanatics marching forward with imperfect unity. All of them did not have the same thoughts but they all shouted the same slogans. Some of them were perpetually fighting, working, and persecuting while others were perpetually winning.

✦ 118 ✦

MADAM MOHINI - A Romantic Tale of Violence

I cursed the mission. I loathed their slogan. It was going from one lie to another. I cursed it because it had taken away my parents; it had turned me into a pebble on the road. People kicked and trampled it. There were many more pebbles like me, though I could not see them, I felt them and knew that they too were in pain. At that time, I could even feel their pain. But as the years passed, I learnt that you simply must know that people are in pain but you must not feel the pain. This unfeelingness automatically enhances your chances of survival. You don't have to go to school to learn this. People teach you and life teaches you. See, I have learnt it so perfectly now.'

Madam paused and looked at Sukhbir and said, 'This is why it is only you and me in this room,' she sighed inaudibly.

'Of course,' Sukhbir answered solemnly.

'At this time, I can't remember when he had come to Gursimran's house for the first time. But I have a feeling that I had heard his name earlier than I remember seeing him. He was called Jinda. He mostly accompanied Sukkha but sometimes he would come alone as well. They looked very much alike; the same small eyes and big turbans. When I had noticed for the first time, I had felt a kind of shudder in my bones — both of them had the same remarkable flash in their eyes and both of them spoke with the same passion in their voice. I guessed at once, I don't know what made me guess, that he too would perish.

✦ 119 ✦

MADAM MOHINI - A Romantic Tale of Violence

Though the dates and times have got blurred, I remember it was the rainy season of 1986. Jinda, Sukkha, and five more men were engaged in a serious calculation that evening. I could not manage to enter the hearing zone. Even Gursimran was excluded from the discussions which suggested the top-secret nature of the meeting. At the most, I could only hear a few words — KCF, Pune, AV — and some more words which I don't remember now. It appeared as if they were engaged in some fresh conspiracy. I couldn't hear much but I could see a lot and could feel even more.

Uncontrollable exclamations of rage were breaking out of the faces of the people in the room. Sukkha was kicking his heel violently against the floor. In another half an hour, an ecstasy of fear and vindictiveness, a desire to kill, to smash faces seemed to flow through the whole group like an electric current. It seemed impossible for the others to avoid joining it. The whole atmosphere was charged. Some had joined just to push some of the others deeper into the bog of hatred. Nonetheless, everyone joined ultimately. Jinda's face turned bright pink when he shouted, 'Khalistan Zindabad'. All shouted behind him. Such is the power of hate. People join much faster when their hate is invoked than their love. Wherever there is love there is hate. But where love makes you weak, hate makes you strong. They are not contradictory but complementary.

After some hours, four men including Jinda and Sukkha, left with two huge bags. The three who were

MADAM MOHINI - A Romantic Tale of Violence

left behind took their turns to the bedroom, had some drinks, and left late at night.

I don't remember all the people who visited that house but one more stands out distinctly in my memory. He looked monstrous at that time. He had a black curly beard and protuberant lips. I saw him in that house only twice. I remember him clearly because I see him almost every week now. His picture hangs in my office where I see him daily. He is a crumbling man now, but at that time he was immensely strong. Now his great body is sagging, sloping, and falling away. He might be in his early fifties those days. He would leave as furtively as he came. It was ensured that not even a fly should see him. His gunmen were also in civil clothes and followed him like his shadow. He is our honourable Chief Minister now. He is a great man and I can go on praising him endlessly.'

She paused and poured herself some water.

'But since it is only you and me, I can confide. This is a piece of abstract evidence which is a fragment of an abolished past. It was a conversation between Gursimran, Billa, and the now CM which I heard. Though this piece of evidence exists nowhere outside my memory it had once existed. This piece of evidence is enough to blow the party to atoms if it is ever known to the world. But I can't let this happen as it would be like drilling holes into the ship I am sailing on.

'Are they happy now?' The now CM asked expressionlessly. Keeping his face flat had never been

MADAM MOHINI - A Romantic Tale of Violence

difficult for him. He could even control his breathing with some effort. But how could one control the beating of one's heart? So, it could clearly be felt that his heart was knocking at his ribs. He pushed back his chair to get as far away as possible from the two men sitting in front of him.

'They need money and if you continue providing that you are safe,' Billa said in a voice nearing a whisper. 'Sahib, you have no dearth of money and you know how you entered their hit-list and these men keep their promises... well,' he paused, '...almost always.'

Gursimran sat mutely staring at their faces in turns, like an owl. The now CM's face stiffened, perhaps in an effort to ward off any signs of fear appearing thereof.

'Now I am doing whatever they want,' he said in a suitably plain voice. 'Have you made sure that no accident will happen?' he added, adjusting his spectacles on his nose. Because of the angle at which he was sitting, his spectacles caught no light and they looked like two black discs on his eyes. Gursimran seemed to be eagerly agreeing with everything that the now CM said. He repeatedly kept remarking, 'You are so right.' He sounded stupidly flattering.

'Don't worry, sahib; as long as I am there your safety is my responsibility,' Billa sounded confident. His confidence gave the now CM a momentary relief. He stood up to leave. I saw a dizzy restlessness in the movements of his body while he was going. He is a...'

+ 122 +

MADAM MOHINI - A Romantic Tale of Violence

Madam began to say something but then stopped hesitantly. There was something on the tip of her tongue, but she checked herself, not fully certain about the safety of that remark or even if she should say it. The now CM's face floated into her mind. The party tells you to reject the evidence your eyes see and your ears hear. This is their final and most essential command. It is a solid world of politics where the laws do not change. They had been the same from forever to forever. The most important of all the laws is to *save your life and to save your chair*. And the second most important is if *the party announces that one plus one is three then it is three. No questions asked!*

'I don't hold him wrong in reaping the harvest sown by the militants,' Madam said trying to convince herself of the logic of her loyalty, 'someone had to do it. What does it matter if he did?' She quickly returned to her story to avoid thinking more about the CM.

'It was a lonely hour of another dark night. Most probably, it was mid-September and the year was certainly 1986. Four men were sitting in silence, a plate of fruit in front of them, they were Jinda, Gursimran, Billa, and another man whose name I don't remember. They sat almost motionless, not speaking a word. The sky had been overcast for the last four days which made everything look grey. Even the leaves of the rose bushes planted in the backyard stopped looking green. It seemed to be drizzling forever. Every stone, every brick,

✦ 123 ✦

MADAM MOHINI - A Romantic Tale of Violence

and every speck of soil was drenched to its soul. There were puddles of muddy water everywhere on the street. The gutter outside the house was overflowing with a black coloured liquid which let out a smell of rotting urine and dead rats.

A draught of wind brought that strong smell of filth into the room where these men were sitting. Gursimran twitched his nose but the other three men never even stirred or noticed. When I got a chance, I glanced at Jinda's face. His face looked ruined and he had tears in his eyes. I shuddered. Something was seriously wrong. Suddenly and strangely, I started feeling unsafe in that house. That is when it struck me that the most horrible thing about staying in that house was not its cruelty but the insecurity. If Jinda's eyes were tearful because a disaster had happened, it was not a thing to worry about. But if the tears indicated an impending disaster, I had to plan to leave that house fast. Terrifying memories rushed into my mind like a hurricane. The smell of burning flesh came back and Mani's screams bruised my ears. Horrors of the refugee camp flashed through my eyes like a film playing in fast-forward mode.

I spent that night in absolute panic caused by the impossibility of knowing what would happen to me next. The sweat started from my backbone. My bones trembled at short intervals with the horrible pangs of terror. The pangs, even when subsided, left a sort of uneasiness. Sleep finally overcame my overworked

MADAM MOHINI - A Romantic Tale of Violence

nerves for some hours. When I got up, everything was normal. Nothing seemed abnormal or out of place. I was extremely relieved.

Later in the morning when the milkman came, I went out to take milk. I saw three men standing very close together in the middle of the street. The middle one was holding a newspaper which the other two were trying to read over his shoulder. One of them was a Hindu. It was obvious that they were reading a serious piece of news. I got curious and started moving closer to them. I was a few paces away when suddenly the group broke up and two of them got into a violent argument. They were almost ready to come to blows. Then the Hindu man received a punch on his jaw from the other man. The third tried to intervene and push them apart. A crowd started gathering. Some of them were watching the scuffle, some wanted to know the cause while a few tried to pacify the belligerent parties. The angry duo was sent back into their houses but the crowd stayed on and discussed the issue for a long time.

From their talk, I came to know the reason for yesterday's pall of gloom. Sukkha had been arrested in Pune after a high-profile assassination. I also came to know the degree to which the passions of the common people had been affected. Though the fight between two men that I had just witnessed retained the characteristics of a street brawl — two men trying to hit each other and both providing special sound effects with popular

✦ 125 ✦

abuses and one or two other men pulling them apart, but it had attained a religious colour, which was not there till a few years back.

* * * * * * *

Many months passed by without anything substantial taking place which could retain itself in my memory. Winter ensued and New Year arrived with no promises. During the second month of the New Year, one evening, I remember there was hectic activity in the house. The main door opened and closed many times. And late in the evening, Jinda came in a jeep. He dragged two big sacks inside. After which he held a hurried conversation with Gursimran. I came to know that they had robbed a bank named PNB in Ludhiana. And those bags had the loot in them.

'We are going to Jammu and will be back in two weeks to take this stuff,' Jinda informed Gursimran, who was nodding his head to emphasise his agreement with whatever he was saying.

'Till then it is your responsibility, this is Rs 5.7 crores.' Then he puffed his chest with pride and uttered the slogan, *'Bole So Nihal...'* then both of them said in unison, *'Sat Siri Akal.'* And he left in his jeep.

Gursimran opened one sack and his eyes brightened with an unprecedented light. It was a lot of money, so much that he had never expected to see even in his

MADAM MOHINI - A Romantic Tale of Violence

wildest dreams. Then his eyes grew curiously suggestive. They flitted nervously from side to side. I felt an urge surging up in me — an urge to have a look at the contents of the sacks. But it would be unwise to go into that room unless I had some definite business. I frantically searched my mind to find an excuse for walking into that room. But before I could think of any, the sacks were no longer there. Without wasting any time, they had been hidden somewhere. Then I heard some hushed voices from his bedroom. Gursimran and his wife were having some kind of whispered discussion. He emerged from the room after almost an hour with one bag in each of his hands. He slipped the bags under the rear seat of his car and drove away.

An uneasy peace descended on the house. No one ate dinner. Pammi was pacing up and down, leaving one room, entering another. Jeetu was jumping behind her. She seemed to be packing some things. I sat in a corner of the lobby and kept on watching her with edified boredom. I could not figure out much but I was aware that in some way she had her hands full. I thought about her and it suddenly struck me that she was exceptionally stupid and had an absolutely empty mind. There was not a single thought in her mind which could actually differentiate her from an animal. Suddenly, she yelled at Jeetu and asked him to disappear. After some time, he popped up behind me with a toy gun aimed at me. He made a vicious gesture. I felt disgusted. Then

MADAM MOHINI - A Romantic Tale of Violence

he started leaping around me, screaming and yelling. It was slightly frightening. His mother barked again. This time at me.

'Get up and pack your stuff.' She shouted.

'Pack what?' I was shocked and taken aback.

'Are you deaf or what? I said PACK,' she yelled.

Gursimran returned in the dead of the night but he was not alone. There was a police jeep accompanying him. It was an entirely abnormal thing. I was scared out of my life. But the scare left me as soon as I saw no fear on Gursimran's face. Everything else went on unsaid. Pammi quickly loaded the car with the luggage she had just packed. Gursimran threw Jeetu in the back seat and pushed me in too. Pammi managed to stuff herself in the front of the car with little space for Gursimran's hand to change gears. The house was locked and we left for an undisclosed location. The Police escorted us. After an hour, we ended up in a small house on a narrow street. There were houses all around. It didn't even seem to be the same town.

'Where are we?' I asked hesitatingly.

'Khamano,' he replied.

My heart sank. I had never heard this name before. Actually, I was not bothered about that at all. What I was really bothered about was that I was no longer in Patiala and that made my heart sink. The place looked like a dirty brown slum. The cobbled street had single-storey houses with battered doors. Open drains ran

MADAM MOHINI - A Romantic Tale of Violence

along both sides of the street, overflowing with filth and inhabited by thousands of happy families of mosquitoes and house flies. The houses had people in astonishing numbers — swollen women, old bent creatures, and barefooted children jumping in puddles of dirty water. Most of the windows in the street were broken and covered with old ragged jute sacks.

Old men and women sat in doorways almost all day long, eyeing everything and everyone with boredom. Some of the swollen women could always be found talking in the street at any time of the day. They enthusiastically engaged in high pitch haggling with the vegetable vendors who sold tired-looking vegetables every day. They studied me in hostile silence whenever I happened to go past them. Gursimran and his wife never left the house. Not even peeped out of a window. All the outdoor work was completely on me.

In the evening, there would be commotion in the whole street. Children and women could be heard yelling from every side. Sometimes a young woman would leap out of a doorway to grab a child playing in a puddle and leap back again. At the sight of a plane in the sky, the children would let out excited screams and point to the sky in unison.

It was a primitive place, even more, primitive than my village. It was full of ugliness. Nearly everyone was ugly. Women dressed up in the most unaesthetic colours. Some had crudely lipsticked mouths and loads

MADAM MOHINI - A Romantic Tale of Violence

of red in their partings as aggressive symbols of their lost virginity. The stinging brightness of the colours that they chose to wear made me feel colour nauseated. The men, on the other hand, chose colours that were impossible to put in any category other than brown - brownish grey, greyish-brown, yellowish-brown, and so on.

It was a dingy, decaying street that always smelt of bad lavatories and rags. I wanted to run away from there. But I had begun to realize that somehow my fate had been written along with that of Gursimran's family, though like a postscript.

Almost a month went by. One day, there was a mood of celebration in the house. Gursimran and Pammi had brightened up. Gursimran was muttering, 'Thank you, Waheguru,' repeatedly and overwhelmingly. Pammi was laughing involuntarily and saying, 'We are free'. She kept repeating it again and again as if she could not believe it. Her fat face became pink with a sudden rush of blood when she suddenly screamed and said, 'We are rich and we are free'. Jeetu was leaping around them cheerfully, not knowing exactly why. I too, felt a faint feeling of satisfaction even though not knowing what had actually happened. I came to know about it only when I read the newspaper. Jinda had been caught by the police from a Gurudwara in Delhi. My heart quailed for a brief second. But the next second it gladdened at the possible conclusion that I would be finally out of

✦ 130 ✦

that slum now. And just as I had expected and hoped, it happened the next week.

Thereafter, things changed fast.'

* * * * * * *

Chapter 6

A brutal smile appeared on Madam's face and within no time it was in full bloom. Sukhbir distinctly remembered this smile of hers. She had given the same smile when Sukhbir had handed her the newspaper one calm morning. Slanting rays of the sun glided onto the ground.

'Good!' she said flashing an applauding glance at him.

'A car accident...hmm...sounds perfectly unplanned and that too with a truck, perfectly normal. Well done, Sukhbir.' She praised him.

She thought again, this time with some sadness, although she knew that that journalist was fully capable of exposing her.

'There was something subtly wrong with him. Though he worked sincerely but with a sort of stupid zeal which made him find out things, which were better hidden. He lacked something which made for survival.

MADAM MOHINI - A Romantic Tale of Violence

So he had to die. It was part of the unavoidable order of things,' she sighed resignedly.

* * * * * * *

Madam went to the small round tea table which sat in one corner of the room. A salad of fresh lettuce and black olives was laid on the table in a crystal bowl. A look at the succulent green of the lettuce made her feel good and happy. Suddenly, the oval olives reminded her of hollowed eye sockets of a skull. She looked away with a jerk. Sukhbir served the salad for both of them. While eating, she looked into her doll's black-button eyes. They seemed to sparkle like twin stars.

Immediately a delicate thought replaced all the harsh and hard thoughts spinning in her head. It occurred to her that now was the time to put everything aside and move on. It was time to pour out all the pent-up feelings and relax. The warm dim light of the table lamp rendered a placidity to the air. She felt with some certainty that it was good to sit in the room like this, utterly secure with nobody overhearing her and no sounds except the friendly ticking of the clock. And to speak out all those memories which had been pricking her soul like needles for so many years.

* * * * * * *

MADAM MOHINI - A Romantic Tale of Violence

Somewhere, a dog barked ferociously and many more joined him in a chorus creating quite a din.

'If only one could eliminate these barking bastards,' she murmured beneath her breath.

On her orders, hordes of them had already been picked up and terminated by the municipal committee, yet more came in. They didn't need buses or cars to do that. They simply walked in tempted by the absence of competition for food and sex.

Her mind went back to the thought of relaxing. A half-remembered song ran through her mind. She tried to recall when she had heard it for the first time. It was long back, perhaps on the radio. But in later years she often heard it playing on the expensive music system which Gursimran had brought home. How the song went on she didn't remember, she just knew the first two lines:

Sun charkhey di mitthi mitthi ghook
Mahiya mainu yaad aanvda

It was curious that when she hummed this song to herself, she actually had the illusion of hearing the *'ghook'*. Yet, she could not remember ever having heard that sound.

She grew reminiscent and continued narrating, 'That day, it was after lunch. This song was playing and Jeetu was particularly, by some queer logic, fond

MADAM MOHINI - A Romantic Tale of Violence

of it. He danced vaguely, twisting and turning at his waist, flinging his arms open and swirling around to the beats of the song. Though I never liked him, his dance never failed to amuse me. Sometimes his dumb throat pulsated along with the song to produce sounds but the effort invariably ended in a feeble squeak. He shook his head in frustration but his eyes never stopped gleaming. His spirited carefree movements added spark to the whole atmosphere. And when he fell on his knees and tossed his head from side to side with his face up and eyes closed, I felt an invisible force pulling me and I too felt like joining him in that act of insane head tossing. However, I dared not, for fear of Pammi, who had grown even fatter by then.

I remember, once when she was not at home, I had given in to the pull. To begin with, a hesitation mixed with fear held me back for some time but finally, I broke myself free and started to dance. It took me to a state of absolute elation, with our arms up in the air. We were completely absorbed in the head tossing, oblivious to everything around us. Abruptly there was a hard knock on my head and I was pulled out of elation by a rude jerk. Pammi stood in front of me. My heart turned to ice. For a few seconds, I was too paralysed to move. Her enormous elephantine legs seemed to form a wall of human flesh.

'Have you gone nuts?' she shouted in her peculiar ear-splitting tone. 'He is a little boy but do you have

✦ 135 ✦

MADAM MOHINI - A Romantic Tale of Violence

no sense?' she barked again. I stood on my shaking legs and walked away as fast as I could. My heart was throbbing loudly. Though the fright left me in a few minutes, a nagging uneasiness persisted for long after that. An impotent resentment welled up inside me. Her real objective in shouting at me was not to tell me the lie that he was a little boy. If he were a little boy, I was also a little girl. But that was not the fact. I remember I had already attained puberty at that time, perhaps a year ago. I would have been just fifteen years of age and Jeetu was less than a year younger to me. My dance would not have bothered her had it been a mechanical joyless act. But I dared not dance thereafter.

Pammi seemed invincible. I could not even imagine an open rebellion against her. I could rebel only by secret disobedience or at the most, by isolated acts of violence against Jeetu or by breaking some utensils in the kitchen or by dancing inside my small washroom.

* * * * * * *

The years of plenty had comfortably settled in that house. Gursimran bought some trucks and started a transport agency. The very next year he bought a very big rice shelling unit at Khamano. Day by day, everything was whizzing upwards. Riches kept pouring in which got translated into a big bungalow in Patiala and properties in other cities also. His wife became even

MADAM MOHINI - A Romantic Tale of Violence

more engrossed in shopping and parties. Hardly a day went by without her bringing loads of shopped things. Gursimran now had several employees under him. Some servants were also added to the house — a short Nepali gatekeeper, a lanky dark gardener, a pale and bent washerman. Some other workers also appeared from time to time to run some errands. They were mostly employees in Gursimran's business and were called by Pammi when she thought there was a need.

But the most important to me was an old man, who was in his fifties at that time. One morning, Pammi was sitting in the garden with her eyes dug into a magazine. It was her favourite Hindi monthly which contained nothing except sensational stories oozing sex, crime, and rubbish pieces of news and beauty tips. It was one of those numerous magazines designed to keep such stupid women busy.

Once, I remember, while dusting her bedroom, I had come across a magazine in the bedside drawer. I had looked at the picture on the front page. It was a picture of a nude woman with a heavily painted face who was in a close hug with a nude muscular man. They were not visible below the waist. The woman's breasts were pressed against the man's chest. The title of the cover story ran – *Sex Life Mein Rang Kaise Bharen.* (How to colour your sex life?). For a moment I was tempted to open the magazine to see if there were better nudes, especially of men, but my hands were already trembling

MADAM MOHINI - A Romantic Tale of Violence

with fear. She would smash my skull for opening her drawer. With an involuntary jerk, my hands pushed the magazine back and banged the drawer shut.

So, that day she was sitting in the garden, reading the magazine and sipping tea. I was cleaning the kitchen slab and could watch her through the kitchen window. An old man stood near her with folded hands. He was short, bent, and squarish with mongoloid eyes and a stubby nose. With dark hair and a small mouth, he was at once mournful and derisive. He seemed to be pleading about something. Pammi continued scanning her magazine with feigned indifference. She was not looking at him. The only response she was giving was an intermittent shake of her head.

The old man's monologue continued for half an hour but failed to invoke any verbal response from her. After some time, he stopped, wiped his eyes and started walking tiredly towards the gate. Pammi gave a calculated look at his back and said something. The man turned, hobbled back towards her and fell on her feet. After five minutes, the man was at the kitchen door, accompanied by Pammi.

'He will help you in the kitchen. Teach him the work,' she quaked harshly at me.

My heart sank. *What if he had been brought in to replace me*, was the only thought that filled my mind. I gave him a hostile look from head to toe. His clothes were dirty. His shirt hung loosely on his shoulders and his

✦ 138 ✦

MADAM MOHINI - A Romantic Tale of Violence

trousers finished just before his ankles started. His dark ugly feet looked disgusting in the large oversized V-shaped slippers. His face was tanned and devastated. He seemed tamable and harmless. He greeted me with a feeble smile. I smiled back reluctantly. Beads of sweat stood out all over his face. The acrid stench of his sweat filled my nostrils.

'Look at yourself. You are as dirty as a pig,' I said with an air of superiority. 'Have you brought clothes?' I raised my voice to assert my seniority.

He nodded miserably. It was on the tip of my tongue to say, 'Ok, uncle, first sit and relax,' but I checked myself, not sure if that sympathetic remark would not in some way dilute my authority.

'Then go, take a shower, change and then come back,' I maintained the sternness of my tone.

'Where?' he uttered lamely.

'This is not for me to tell. Go and ask the gatekeeper,' I said, pretending to be busy in peeling garlic.

He left.

I smiled inwardly. This was, quite relieving. The kind of relief which one gets when one pees after compulsorily holding it for many hours. At last, I had someone at whom I could also shout and be rude. It was interesting. He was far older than me and I did not have even the faintest idea of who he was. Yet, an inexplicable easiness was caused by his arrival. I felt a strange hatred for him. Perhaps, it was the natural hatred one servant has for the other.

✦ 139 ✦

MADAM MOHINI - A Romantic Tale of Violence

He worked diligently in the kitchen — chopping the vegetables and cooking to perfection. Initially, I avoided talking to him. Whenever he tried to talk to me, I snubbed him or left the kitchen. But it all started one day when he kept his hand on my head and said that his daughter was of my age. Instinctively, I looked into his eyes. They were wet with unshed tears.

'What happened to her?' I asked pretending to be least interested.

'She died,' his throat was choked and he blinked to clear his eyes. I immediately looked away so as to hide the expression of pity welling up in my eyes but I couldn't stop myself from asking, 'How?' So he told me that one night a fire consumed his house as well as his daughter and wife. I kept my eyes fixed on his grim face. Tears rolled down his pale cheeks.

As it turned out, both of us started mixing up well. I started calling him Bahadur uncle. To begin with, it was harmonious cooperation at work. Gradually, he took over almost all the work and would not let me do much. He did everything — peeling, chopping, cooking, washing, sweeping the kitchen floor, cleaning the slabs — always slowly with a curious lack of superfluous motion. I kept sitting or standing in the kitchen idly talking to him.

Such a time had come to me after years, the years which had once seemed eternal. Life ceased to be horrifying. I started feeling the warmth of my mother's

✦ 140 ✦

MADAM MOHINI - A Romantic Tale of Violence

body in his hug. After work was over, we would slowly stroll down the lawn. One day he held my hand with a curious disarming friendliness and asked casually, 'Where are your parents?' My heart stirred painfully. The bareness, dinginess, and listlessness of my life struck me in my face as if someone had slapped me. The past flashed before my eyes and I realised that certain things just can't be erased from memory. Some voices started raising their head, enveloping my mind.

'She is hiding somewhere I don't know where?' I answered softly.

'Who?' He asked curiously.

'My mommy. To this day, I don't know where she is. It is possible that she is doing all this for me,' I sighed deeply.

'And your Dad?' He sounded concerned.

'I don't know. He too, disappeared during those times, the times of great purges. Perhaps he is no more. But she is there, somewhere, I can feel her breath in the air.' I told him with conviction.

We continued to stroll on the lawn. A mysterious quiet had descended over us. The quiet was brutally disturbed by the barking of Pammi. She needed tea immediately.

He never talked about my family thereafter.

A month went by. One day Bahadur uncle told me to manage the work as he had to go to the market. He returned in the evening. When the house had settled for

✦ 141 ✦

the night, he quietly came to my room. He startled me by giving me a big bundle of books.

'Today, I got my first salary. I have bought books for you,' he said casually.

'I wanted my daughter to study. Will you do it on her behalf?' he took a deep deliberative breath. I kept on staring at him in gaping surprise. A powerful mix of emotions confused me. I didn't know how to react. I found myself close to tears. It seemed like a luminous dream in which my whole life stretched out before me like a beautiful landscape with flowers and butterflies. I saw my mother standing amidst the flowers, making a protective gesture with her arms.

Bahadur uncle sat beside me and his body relapsed into stillness. For some infinite minutes, we just sat almost immobile. I remembered my mother's statuesque body bending over the gas stove to stir something in the saucepan. I saw myself clinging to her like a baby monkey and looking at the world from over her shoulders.

'I am waiting for something which I know should happen,' I muttered faintly.

Bahadur uncle put his hand around my shoulders and said, 'She will be happy to see you an educated girl. She won't have any regrets then.'

What overwhelmed me at that moment was admiration for the gesture with which he had gifted me the books. He was a small frail figure. The skin of his

MADAM MOHINI - A Romantic Tale of Violence

face was roughened by the sun and blunt razor blades. I felt the comforting cosiness that filled the room due to his presence. The world outside, even through the shut windows and doors, felt cold. There seemed to be no colour in anything except in the books which he had brought. They seemed to belong to that vanished romantic past where everything was colourful.

My heart gladdened and expanded and I happily clutched the books. I had forgotten most of what I had learnt in school and as I looked at the titles of the books, I realised I could hardly read. I had been good at studies but I tried not to think of school or the day I left it or any part of my childhood. I resolved that nothing will stop me now. I focussed my mind and began to work at reading the titles: *Supplementary reader-class X*. I managed to read one and got excited. I looked at him with bright eyes. He was charmed. I hugged the books to myself and felt a strange strength. The books were of the Punjab school education board's syllabus for class X. I could be a matriculate if I passed the class X examination from open school. This programme had been designed to bring the dropouts back to mainstream education. Bahadur's presence in the kitchen was already giving me plenty of spare time, some part of which invariably went into Jeetu's tantrum management plus unexpected calls from his mother. I could use the rest of it to study.

I took on the new books one by one. I read haltingly. To my dismay, I found that there were many words of

MADAM MOHINI - A Romantic Tale of Violence

English that I could barely read. And when I worked hard, pieced together the letters, and constructed the words, they produced only hollow sounds. I couldn't understand what they meant. I was totally disheartened. I sat there staring at the pages of a book wondering if I would ever be able to read and understand them. A vision of Bahadur's hopeless eyes stung my conscience and I was determined to try again.

I started working on my books. My head ached with the effort. But I was resolute and didn't let my mind wander. I stayed in my room for hours together, labouring over the books, took short breaks, then went back to the books again. After some days of labour, I found that even though I could decipher many words yet it was a struggle to find out what they meant. I remained confused. Old skills of reading and writing were slowly coming back but it was not enough to pass the matriculation examination.

It was with great difficulty that I kept myself from quitting. Bahadur uncle's face swam into my mind — heavy, calm, and hopeful. It was more difficult to disappoint him than to slog at the books. I tried again, this time with little more success than before. I opened another book. It was a history book. The first Chapter was titled "The Stone Age". It had taken me almost the whole day to read that one. I understood nothing. I took a deep breath and started reading again. The second attempt tasked my nerves. I was completely baffled by now. It was dark outside. I was tired and my neck and shoulders were aching. I stared into space wondering what to do? A sense of helplessness took hold of me. Suddenly, the books seemed nothing but a heap of rubbish. One could read them the whole life without getting any real knowledge.

The next morning, I woke up late. My head felt heavy. I secretly threaded my way towards the kitchen so that no one would know that I had woken up so late. A hum of murmuring voices was coming from Gursimran's office room which was nearest to the kitchen. I saw some men hurrying to and fro in the corridor. I didn't know their names though I had often seen them in the house. They always looked very political in their white overalls and blue turbans. These were usually the pre-breakfast or the post-dinner guests.

I reached the kitchen. Bahadur uncle was squatting in one corner on the floor with a cup of tea in his hand. As soon as he saw me, he poured tea for me as well which he had saved out of the tea made for the guests. I took the cup of tea and squatted in front of him. Neither of us spoke till we had finished our tea. As soon as I opened my mouth to speak, he stood up nimbly to work on the breakfast. I thought for a while then stood behind him. He was making dough for *paranthas*. We were not face-to-face so I spoke. I said it all. All that was in my mind and all that I was having difficulty with. He looked meditatively at the big ball of dough.

MADAM MOHINI - A Romantic Tale of Violence

He went to the sink to wash his hands and finished washing them slowly. I got impatient in the absence of any verbal response.

'Perhaps, I have not made myself clear,' I said.

No response came.

'What I am trying to say is that you have been alive for a very long time. What would you say, from what you remember, that life would be any better than now if I study?'

At last, he stirred. 'I know what you expect me to say,' he said with a tolerant philosophical air, 'you have your strength when you are young and when you get to my time in life, you will realise what I mean.'

I sat back against the wall. There was no use going on. He shuffled rapidly towards the iron basket which contained potatoes, took about ten out of them and pushed them towards me and said, 'Boil these'. I sat for a minute or two gazing at the potatoes. I didn't notice when he left the kitchen. I stood up and put the potatoes in the pressure cooker, filled it with the requisite amount of water, and put it on the burner. I started thinking about the question I had posed to him. Though it was simple, it was huge. In fact, it was unanswerable. It is unanswerable even today. People are made to remember a million useless things but the relevant knowledge is kept outside the range of their vision. This is well contrived.

My train of thought was interrupted by his return. He walked in with a spring in his step. His face was

MADAM MOHINI - A Romantic Tale of Violence

flushed. He caught me gently by my arm and said, 'Every problem has a solution,' he sounded extremely excited. 'I talked to *Shaabji*. He is ready to get a tutor for you.' I stood looking at him for an instant. A smile started to appear at the corners of my mouth but it was suddenly nipped by a thought, 'But... but who will pay for it.'

'I will...I told him I will,' he said confidently.

* * * * * * *

It was the middle of the morning. I had left the kitchen to play cricket with Jeetu who wanted to play just then, without any delay. My head always went numb with boredom when he asked for it. But to play and let him win was one of my compulsory duties. He had to be made to hit a six at every ball and his mad yells had also to be patiently tolerated.

While we were playing, we saw a solitary figure coming towards us from the other end of the lawn. He was a thin tall man with dark hair. As he came nearer, I saw that he was a young boy with a hooked nose on which his spectacles were perched. He resettled his spectacles on his nose in a curiously civilised way. Something in his face suggested intelligence. At any rate, he had the appearance of being someone I would like to talk to. He was coming towards me. My heart bumped.

'I am Amrit. I am your tutor.' He introduced himself as soon as he reached me.

An involuntary squeak of surprise escaped my throat.

♦ 147 ♦

MADAM MOHINI - A Romantic Tale of Violence

'Sir has told me to fix a time between lunch and the evening tea so your household work is not hampered in any way.' He continued talking to me.

I nodded. Jeetu felt neglected. He started shouting irregular syllables and kicking his heel violently against the ground. I gave Jeetu an angry flash of my eyes and looked at Amrit again. I was trying to form words in my mind to say something decent but by the time I reached the moment of speaking, Jeetu's anger had flared up. He sprang towards me with his bat to smash my face.

I jumped away just in time to save myself. Amrit got alarmed. He looked disturbed. But it was a normal occurrence for me. I stood there calmly. Momentarily, I caught his eye. He had taken off his spectacles. His protuberant eyes flitted nervously from side to side. He resettled his spectacles on his nose and said, 'We will start tomorrow with English'. And he left hastily. For that fraction of a second when our eyes had met, I could read in them that he won't come, that he had contempt for violence and will not work under such circumstances. A fresh wave of hatred for Jeetu gripped my mind and I felt like crushing his skull. I wanted to flog him to death and then cut his throat with my kitchen knife.

That was all. I was already uncertain if something like this had even taken place, and was even more uncertain about his coming the next day. I sat in one corner of my room that night. I wanted to try to read the books again. I picked up the English textbook. It

✦ 148 ✦

MADAM MOHINI - A Romantic Tale of Violence

was a beautiful book. Its smooth creamy paper looked romantic. For some time, I sat gazing stupidly at the paper, at the book. My mind went back to Amrit. I was sure he would not come. My diaphragm constricted at the thought. I refocused my eyes on the page of the book. It looked absurd and useless. I slapped the book close and flung it away.

* * * * * * *

The next morning was a usual one. Bahadur uncle and I were engaged in the kitchen. I hesitated for some time but finally gave way to my impulse and asked him about Amrit. 'Who is that boy who is coming to teach me?'

'He is *Shaabji's* accountant's relative,' he informed me. He further added that he was a poor boy who needed money to continue his studies. He was to take the 12th class examination that year.

'It needs desperate courage to defy the treacheries of luck,' he said solemnly, 'only unrelenting people can do it.' I kept staring at his face as he spoke. Then after some moments, I asked him quietly, 'Will he come today?'

'Yes, why not?' he answered promptly. In some ways, he was more acute and far less susceptible to negative thoughts than me. He had an incredible capacity to live on and remain positive.

I waited for my teacher after lunch. I looked around my shabby little room. I heard someone singing outside the window. I peeped out. No one was there. The sun

♦ 149 ♦

MADAM MOHINI - A Romantic Tale of Violence

was still high in the sky. Summer was at its peak. The year was 1990. It was the hottest sleepiest hour of the afternoon. The sun blazed down at everything. I waited for one hour. My thoughts were all based on that one moment when our eyes had met, beyond that were only my own secret imaginings. Teenage, as they call it, makes you prone to think vaguely.

I was almost certain by then that he won't turn up. I went to bed and decided to stop thinking about him. Sleep overcame me. I was startled out of my sleep by a knock at the door. For a moment, I was seized by a kind of hysteria. I was not allowed to sleep during the afternoons. It must be Pammi to thrash me for sleeping. The worst thing would be delay in opening the door. My heart started thumping loudly like a drum. I got up and jumped towards the door, drew in my breath, and opened it. Instantly, a warm wave of relief swept through my body. It was Amrit.

'Sorry, I got late. My cycle's tyre got punctured on the way.' His face was red due to the heat of the sun. My face would have looked expressionless as it always does when I try to hide a very strong emotion.

'Are you ready to start?' he asked softly.

My tongue worked soundlessly to form some words. It appeared that a long time passed before I answered. At last, I could only manage to utter a 'YES!'

* * * * * * *

MADAM MOHINI - A Romantic Tale of Violence

As it happened, he taught me seriously for the next six months. Powered by his presence, I discovered a vigorous zest for learning. I soaked up the lessons, immersing myself in those books. I mastered the alphabets and learned to read effortlessly. I slowly understood, though after a lot of slogging, the lifeless principles of mathematics. My teacher was all praise for me; pointing time and again at the quickness of my learning. But I felt it was the result of his keenness.

Whenever I was not up to the expected mark, he spoke to me in his controlled low-pitched voice with a refined precision that reduced me to tears. At other times, he was a dreamy creature with hairy arms. He had a surprising talent with rhymes and literature. My eyes would linger on his face when he read poetry. If he happened to notice, I pretended to be concentrating deeply on the poem. I could not understand all the words of the poems but they conjured up pictures in my head, of wonderful fields and serene rivulets, of butterflies, pastures, and daffodils.

He was quite stern and honest to a fault. It was almost impossible to distract him from a lecture and engage him in short personal talks. But I kept looking for opportunities to do so. And from the few that I could manage, I came to know that the boy was an orphan. His father used to work in a factory on the outskirts of Patiala. One night, when he was going to work by bus for his night shift, the bus was stopped by some armed men. They picked up some people from the bus and killed them. His father was one of them. It happened during those same days, the days of purges when my parents disappeared.

When his father died, his mother did not show any violent grief but a sudden change came over her. She became completely spiritless. Finally, she took a fatal leap into the swollen canal. Committing suicide had almost become a way of life those days. Taking one's own life was viewed as an honourable solution to a wide range of life's problems. I felt pity for him. Both his parents had died. *At least my mummy was alive. She didn't commit suicide. She was brave enough to face anything*, I thought to myself.

One afternoon, he was reading aloud from the science book. It was the last lesson of that book. After completing he shut the book with a snap and looked at my face. His eyes stayed on my face for some seconds longer than usual. 'Do you have any questions?' he asked softly.

I shook my head.

'The syllabus is over. Your exams will start in two months from now,' he paused for a while, 'Now, it is up to you to revise everything yourself,' he said avoiding to look at me this time.

'Will you not come now?' I asked timidly. My heart was beating faster.

He cleared his throat and said, 'No.'

MADAM MOHINI - A Romantic Tale of Violence

My heart pounded violently. He glanced out of the window at the fading light and stood up silently. I was stunned as though it was unexpected. I found myself incapable of uttering any word. He turned around and walked away. I watched him go down the corridor. A forceful desire surged up in me and I wanted to run and catch up with him. But my body seemed to have gone lifeless; it felt paralysed with pain and I stood rooted to the spot. I stared wretchedly after him. A horrifying wave of despair rose within me and my vision got blurred.

All these months, I had waited every day for him with a steadfast conviction that one look into my eyes and he would know, just as I had known from the moment I saw him for the first time- that what I felt for him. And then, possessed with an impulse, my feet were moving before any thought had fully formed in my head. I quickly looked around the house and down the corridor. No one was in sight. Picking up the fall of my *salwaar*, I flew after him; oblivious of anything around. My *dupatta* was flying over my shoulders. I vaguely guessed which direction he might have taken and bolted towards that. I was wearing a red *salwaar-kameez* with a red dupatta. Pammi had worn this dress for many years and had finally given it to me on Jeetu's birthday. I had got it altered to my size. At last, I saw him cycling down the road.

'Amrit,' I shouted.

He stopped and unmounted from his cycle. He looked at me. I ran towards him. He spoke in a cold

MADAM MOHINI - A Romantic Tale of Violence

voice, 'What do you think you are doing? Don't you realise that you might be thrown out of your job?'

'I don't care,' I was panting.

'You don't care but I do. I can't risk my reputation which fetches me tuition jobs,' he advanced towards me. 'Are you of a low breeding?'

I got furious, 'How dare you speak to me like that,' I glared defiantly at him. For a moment I thought he would turn around and go forever or call me thankless. But then I saw a smile erupting on his lips and the next moment he began to laugh lightly and stroked his head. I opened my mouth to protest but he put a finger on his lips signalling me to be quiet.

'Road is not a good place to talk. Follow me quietly.' He told me softly.

I nodded.

There was a small forest of *kikkar* trees running along the roadside. He parted the bushes and quickly led the way along a narrow track into the wood. I followed him. Then he stopped and turned to face me. I stood before him very upright with a faint smile on my face. We stood staring at each other in the shade of the thin foliage of *kikkar* trees. The sunlight filtering through the leaves was still warm on our faces.

'You are looking like a flash of fire in this,' he said pointing at my dress, and then paused. 'So why did you come behind me?' his voice was husky.

✦ 154 ✦

MADAM MOHINI - A Romantic Tale of Violence

I flushed, 'Do you have something to say to me?' I asked tremulously.

He looked down and then taking a deep breath, adjusted his spectacles on his nose, and said, 'Yes...I... we...there can be nothing between us.'

A pain knifed through me.

'But why? Don't you like me?' I asked torturously.

He laughed lightly. 'I have yet to study for many years. Such things distract you from your aim. Moreover, we are very young. I am just 18 and you, I guess 16. You must study too.' He explained patiently.

I was silent for a while and then smiled. 'I will wait.'

Hope blazed across his face for an instant and then he shook his head. I stepped closer to him so that I could feel the heat of his body. His shoulders tensed. 'You are the one for me,' I said quietly. 'Will we not see each other?' I asked.

He raised his hand to my face, 'We will. Who will teach you for your next class?'

I smiled delightedly.

'But for that, you must pass this class,' he said prosaically. My eyes filled with sudden tears, surprising even myself.

The sun slipped further and mating calls of peacocks filled the woods.

'Go now, lest you should be in trouble,' he said firmly.

I nodded. Suddenly the fear of Pammi gripped my mind. I ran back, my heart racing. I slipped into the

✦ 155 ✦

MADAM MOHINI - A Romantic Tale of Violence

house from the back door which opened on the back lawn. A clothesline had washed clothes hung for drying up. I immediately started picking up the dried clothes and looked suitably busy. Inside the house, everything seemed normal.

For the rest of the evening, it was very difficult to work. I was not able to focus my mind on any of the nagging jobs. Even harder was to mask the blush on my face or the happiness in my eyes. Suddenly, life was beautiful and seemed more bearable. Excitement was steadily building up in me. I feigned normalcy. But I could feel that my face was aglow and my eyes aflame. Bahadur was dazed when he saw me as if someone had pulled him out of his sleep by flashing a light in his eyes.

'You are looking very...different...' he managed to finally say and I swung my plait and gave a controlled smile, though I wanted to laugh aloud and if possible, let out a scream of excitement. I wanted to dance like Jeetu and perform that insane tossing of the head. My face had gone hot with the effort of controlling myself from doing anything crazy.

Life was good after all. I worked hard for the 10th class examination and scored 58% marks. It was not a very good score but it was more than enough to go to the next class. And that was what my aim was, new class, new syllabus and I would then need a tutor.'

* * * * * * *

Chapter 7

Her eyes ached due to being awake till late at night. Coming out of the chair seemed an arduous physical task. Though she had the right to stop narrating the story when she wanted, she found herself anxious to carry on. In some mysterious way, it was quite relieving.

She climbed out of the chair. Her knees creaked. She was tired but not at all sleepy. She opened the window and sat in the armchair which lay in front of it. The memories revived a feeling, that blissful feeling of being in love that had not yet worn off. A faint breeze from the window played on her cheeks. The feeling fascinated her. She wanted to let it linger in her mind. She wanted to continue relishing it for some more time. It did not bring anything new but it was still fresh and attractive and gave her an inner warmth. She closed her eyes to be closer to those memories. She heard footsteps approaching the door and started out of her chair to open the door. It was Amrit. He dumped his jute bag, in which he always carried books, on the floor. She flung herself into his arms.

MADAM MOHINI - A Romantic Tale of Violence

A knock at the door pulled her out of her dream with a jerk.

Dreams are powerful. They can make you meet even the ones you haven't seen in years, she thought.

Sukhbir opened the door. It was a servant with tea. With every sip of tea, she went deeper into a quiet reverie, into her mind full of memories. Sukhbir watched her and wondered how such a matter-of-fact woman can fall in love.

Sukhbir remembered, a day just before the last assembly elections when she was addressing a rally of people from a makeshift stage. Thousands of people had gathered, mostly poor and illiterate, who are ever ready to visit political rallies for a pittance. The organisers had dutifully loaded the bought audience and unloaded them at the venue of the rally to win their leader's applause. The crowd sat on thin dusty green carpets spread on the ground. A good number of them stood on the fringes of the huge patch of a seated audience.

'God has given me everything, so much so that I can live an easy life, but I am taking pains to change the fate of you people.' She was saying into the mic.

Sukhbir along with two other close aides stood behind her. They immediately burst into a bout of clapping when she said that. It was to stimulate the audience into clapping. And the *wise* crowd had picked up the hint and started clapping. She smiled with satisfaction and continued. 'Look...' she shouted, 'you can see for

MADAM MOHINI - A Romantic Tale of Violence

yourself the amount of progress my constituency has seen. New roads, new bridges and more new projects are being taken up. I will leave no stone unturned to make the lives of my people better.' She paused. She wanted applause. Sukhbir was lost in some thought. But in two seconds he picked up the cue and started clapping frantically. The audience followed.

She puffed her lungs and straightened her shoulders, 'Sisters and brothers,' she moved her arm and shook her hand at them, 'what I can do for you, no one else can.' She flung out her other arm and shook her head, 'You just keep giving me your love and I will continue to serve you better.' The audience appeared to be admiring her gestures as all heads stirred together. She continued speaking. The audience applauded whenever signalled.

In the ragged hedge on the left side of the ground, *kikkar* boughs were swaying lightly with the breeze. Some people were standing in front of the hedge. For an instant, beyond the hedge, she noticed a man standing. He looked unusual but she felt she had seen him before. The man had shabbily cut dirty hair. Dust seemed to be sticking to his greasy-looking beard. He looked filthier than a pig in a ditch. She immediately took her mind off him and continued with her speech which was about to take an important turn and stir some crucial sentiments.

'My Dalit brothers and sisters know that the way I can feel their pain no one else can. After all, I myself am the daughter of a Dalit.'

✦ 159 ✦

MADAM MOHINI - A Romantic Tale of Violence

A large part of the crowd got so overwhelmed at this dialogue that they stood up involuntarily to applause.

She gestured to the crowd to be seated. 'But... but this does not mean that I feel any less for others. I am also a Sikh and all Sikhs are children of Gurus. All of us are brethren.' Another big part of the crowd clapped with vigour.

'BUT...' Now she raised her voice to be heard over the noise caused by clapping, '...BUT, this also does not mean that I feel any less for my Hindu brethren. After all, we all are Punjabis. Our joys and sorrows are common. We are the organs of one body. If any organ is in pain the whole body feels that pain. Let's stand united and work for a new and happy life for all of us.' And then she ended the speech as always, with the promise to turn Punjab into California.

As soon as the speech was over, she dismounted the stage and scuttled away to her car. People, frail, dark, and bent rushed to give applications to Sukhbir. He quickly gathered as many as he could and leapt towards the car. The Carcade set into motion and people rushed to queue up. They pushed and jostled to occupy the position at the beginning of the queue. Once settled, the queue jerked forward slowly. Everyone took the promised money along with the complimentary cup of tea which was actually nothing more than light brown liquid sweetened with loads of sugar.

MADAM MOHINI - A Romantic Tale of Violence

In the car, Sukhbir said, 'Madam, these applications,' while extending his hand full of papers towards her. She gave him a stern look. She seemed tired and irritated.

'Right,' Sukhbir said crisply and tore the papers into pieces and flung them out of the window of the speeding car, they flew off in all directions.

For some reason she found herself thinking of that man behind the hedge.

'I couldn't see his face clearly because of the distance but his hard expression seemed to be telling me to shut up, you fool, you liar, or maybe things ruder than this,' she told Sukhbir.

'He was tall and thin... too filthy to be even substantial. Madam, you are getting prone to illogical anxieties,' Sukhbir chided her gently.

'But,' she spoke again, 'that man gave an impression of being more dangerous than most.' *Forget...* she commanded her mind.

'There are always thousands of eyes watching you. You can't scrutinise all of them,' Sukhbir replied.

She drew in a deep breath, 'What worried me was the curious intensity with which he was looking at me. He carried with him a suggestion of having something to hide, perhaps, a coincidence.'

Sukhbir listened attentively to her. Then she fell silent for some seconds. A thought was spreading its icy hands on her mind. Suddenly, she said 'Sukhbir, I have the feeling that I have seen him before. The faint image

✦ 161 ✦

of the man who was peeping over the boundary wall last night slightly matched the image of this man.'

'Perhaps, Madam,' Sukhbir said thoughtfully.

'Find out.' She ordered him.

'Yes, Madam.' Sukhbir knew better than to argue with her.

'What is next?' She asked impatiently.

'Madam, you have to join the inauguration of the Sikh Heritage Study Centre at 4:00 pm.'

'I must speak to CM sahib about this.' She said plaintively.

Inside the office, Madam was strolling up and down with her hands locked behind her back. Then she sat down in her chair, thinking deeply. After a few minutes, she turned slightly in her chair to face Sukhbir. He had just finished dialling a phone number from the fixed-line.

'OSD asked me to call in 15 minutes, Madam,' he said promptly.

She stood up and again began to pace slowly, as though she could think better while moving. She looked at her wristwatch again.

'I understand,' she said, 'that I am of no use to the party. They give me orders and I obey them without knowing or asking why? But this is my territory and I am the MLA here. So, why should the SGPC chief be chosen to inaugurate the Sikh Studies Centre?' she rambled agitatedly.

MADAM MOHINI - A Romantic Tale of Violence

'This politics of inaugurations is not a petty thing,' she said, making a universal statement.

'Madam, but I thought that you disliked such inaugurations,' Sukhbir said hesitatingly.

'True, but what else will we inaugurate then? The state does not have money to launch any project other than religious ones. It is only by pretending to be devout Sikhs that we can win votes. Prominent members of the party are already under the cloud for various reasons. There are only a few, who managed,' she paused and adjusted her *dupatta* on her bosom, '...somehow, in whatever way, to maintain an immaculate image. Those of us should be given more and more chances to flash our benevolent faces in the media.' She said grumpily.

She glanced at Sukhbir's face as if waiting for his affirmative response to her assertions. But his face was expressionless. 'Where is this centre? What is it about?' She tried to recall with a casual effort.

Sukhbir gave a prompt reply, 'Centre for Sikh Studies, Madam.'

'Yes. Where is it being opened?' She asked impatiently.

'At Bahadurgarh, Madam,' he replied without much interest.

'Call up now. It's 15 minutes,' she said authoritatively.

Sukhbir quickly began to dial again.

'Hello, Sat Sri Akal Ji,' his lips almost touched the receiver, 'Madam wants to talk to CM Sahib,' his voice was overly oily.

✦ 163 ✦

MADAM MOHINI - A Romantic Tale of Violence

'Yes, please wait,' said the voice on the other side.

Sukhbir handed over the receiver to her and she waited patiently for a few seconds and then, '*Sat Sri Akal*, Sir.' She stood up with militant agility.

'Yes, Biba ji?' the CM queried.

'Sir, I requested that I should be given the opportunity to inaugurate the Sikh Studies Centre at Bahadurgarh,' she said crisply.

'Biba ji, why can't you understand? The calculation is very simple. The day our party loses the confidence of the religious Sikhs, we will be out of power. And the religious Sikhs, who make 90% of the Sikhs and 80% of the total population of our state, are emotionally controlled by SGPC. Inauguration of this centre by the SGPC Chief is a small event but promises us big benefits,' the CM explained extremely politely.

'Yes Sir, but...'

The CM interrupted her before she could complete her sentence, 'Moreover, it is in your constituency so the direct benefit will be reaped by you. Need I remind you from where do you serve 'langar' to the people who gather at your rallies?'

'No, Sir.'

'The SGPC Chief is a kind man. He never thinks twice before feeding the public gathered for our political rallies. We are also invited to address the religious functions organised by SGPC.' The argument was practically profound and politically sound.

✦ 164 ✦

MADAM MOHINI - A Romantic Tale of Violence

Her tongue was working soundlessly; trying to form the opening syllables of one word after another but she could not say anything. The CM stopped abruptly with a final address, 'Sat Sri Akal, Biba Ji.' And he kept the phone with a snap.

She sluggishly kept the receiver back. Sukhbir was looking at her curiously. She cautiously adjusted her dupatta to cover her head and stole a glance at Sukhbir.

'These are petty things and quite worthless too,' she cleared her throat and continued, 'The CM Sahib is right. Only the votes matter.'

There was a pile of files lying on the table awaiting her signatures. She pointed towards them. The gesture meant that Sukhbir should open them one by one and get them signed by her. There were armies of clerks who had toiled over them. She did not need to go through the boring complexities of what was in them.

Moreover, she was one of the directing brains of the party and it was her job to lay down the policy lines. Her other important job was to see where fabrication of facts was required. In that case, the file had to be turned over to a committee. Sometimes the creation of many versions of a fact or set of facts was necessitated. This could be done either to suit her own interests or the interests of some other colleague. This was tedious work and required a sincere worker who would engage in unimaginably intricate distortions to accomplish the task. This task was handled by Sukhbir. She would

MADAM MOHINI - A Romantic Tale of Violence

then select a version and that chosen lie would become a fact.

While doing her job, she took special care, not to incur the displeasure of the party head. People get into the bad books either due to rebellion or for becoming more popular than the head himself. And the people who incurred displeasure would either be expelled from the party or died in road accidents. Therefore, she always maintained a delicate balance and strictly smothered any heretical tendencies. Suddenly the image of a minister who had recently died in a road accident sprang to her mind. Cold and sticky sweat erupted in her palms. She kept the pen aside, spread her fingers, and shook her hands to dry the sweat. She rubbed her forehead gently with her index finger to hide if there was any, expression of nervousness on her face. The next moment her face bore a deadpan expression.

Her face was bent down to sign the files. Sukhbir could see the line of her nose. She looked formidable. For almost ten minutes she sat without stirring but continued signing. Suddenly, the expression on her face changed. The flatness passed out as she spoke on the phone with the Director-General of Police. She had a brief conversation with him which seemed inconclusive. She became uncomfortable in her chair. She got out of it and stretched herself luxuriously. Sukhbir could sense that she was now ready to leave the office. He quickly stepped forward, holding an open diary. Before he could

MADAM MOHINI - A Romantic Tale of Violence

say anything, she spoke, 'I am not going to meet anyone now. Handle on your own,' she said in an iron voice.

'Yes, Madam,' he said controlling the smile that was beginning to appear on his face. He liked it whenever she said that as it brought him many chances to get primarily involved in situations that would otherwise be made secondary by her presence. This primary involvement was what brought him wealth and fame. Suddenly, it struck him that he couldn't be present in the legislative assembly on her behalf. As he reminded her of the imminent budget session, she sighed. A dull ache streaked through her head. The memory of the last assembly session and the injury caused by an 'identified flying object' was revived. Instinctively, her hand rose to feel the skin of her forehead to reassure herself that the wound had healed.

She trembled inwardly. Stepping into the assembly hall was not short of jumping into the well of death. Any moment of discord among the parties would see chairs, tables, pots, or whatever was there, flying in the air. And the chances were high that any one of those objects could give you a fatal blow.

'Democracy has brought us freedom, not that freedom has brought us democracy,' she said mournfully.

Sukhbir was brought back to the present by the tinkle of the teacup as she placed it on the table. She had closed her eyes and was resting her head against the wall. Her chin had tipped up, exposing her jaw and

✦ 167 ✦

MADAM MOHINI - A Romantic Tale of Violence

neckline to the moonlight. The fitful light of the moon cast a dim light on the garden below her window.

'I can feel my mother's presence around me. I see myself clad in a white frock with numerous frills, my favourite one. My mother is looking fondly at me. She dabs a smear of kajal behind my ear to ward off the evil eye'.

'I remember how every Sunday morning she would seat herself on the home-woven cotton matt, which had a pattern of red and blue peacocks on it. Then she would place me on her soft comfortable thighs and massage my head with hot mustard oil. I could feel the rhythmic movements of her fingers on my scalp as she massaged. *You are my precious flower bud* my mom would tell me,' She muttered. *My sun, my moon, my lucky star,* she would say. No one has ever loved me like that. She doted on me. *You are spoiling the girl* my father would shout at her. *She will leave us one day for her husband's home* my mother would reply while combing my hair. After doing up my hair to her satisfaction she would bend and kiss the top of my head and say, *Go and play now, but don't spoil your white dress.*

'When there were fights between my mother and father, she would take me onto her lap, perhaps to make me feel less scared. I would bury my face in her neck but would continue to watch my violent father from the corner of my eye. When he looked at me, I would pull a horrid face. He would look at me gravely for a second and then turn back to the fight.

MADAM MOHINI - A Romantic Tale of Violence

I waited for years but slowly gave up hope that my parents would ever be happy with each other. Even as a child, I knew that it was better for them to separate so that both of them could be happy. My mother had also considered this separation, though very weakly, as I heard her talking to my Nani (maternal grandmother) one day. My Nani had come to our house for a short visit. Always clad in creams and whites, she was a tall and graceful woman. Her fair and wrinkled face felt very soft when I kissed her. She always wore big gold rings in her ears. The pierced holes of her ears had turned into long slits with the weight of those rings.

'I don't want to live with this man anymore, Bee Ji,' my mother had said in a low pleading voice. Her eyes were tearful. Nani sat in perplexed silence for a while. She adjusted her cream dupatta over her grey-haired head and then said quietly, 'Which parents would be happy to see their daughter ruin the family name in this manner, abandoning her husband's house. This is your house. Wise women never leave their houses'.

'But, Bee Ji, isn't your house my house?' my mother asked, her eyes filling with tears.

'But, my child,' Nani pressed, 'as a wife you have your duties. Think about your child. Whatever disagreements exist between a husband and wife; why should the child suffer?

'She won't suffer. In fact, she would be better away from her father,' my mother argued though her voice was breaking.

MADAM MOHINI - A Romantic Tale of Violence

Nani fell silent. Every crease on her face seemed to have tensed up. 'Poor girl, I wish you had a brother,' and she broke into tears.

My soft-hearted mother felt guilty and patted Nani's arm affectionately, 'Bee ji, stop crying. I am sorry I made you weep,' she said meekly. Nani recomposed herself and wiped her old eyes with the end of her dupatta.

'Neither have you got a brother nor a son. For how long will your father live? What will you do when we are dead,' two more tears fell from her eyes, 'A woman needs a man's support and protection to live a graceful life. You have no option other than staying with your husband,' and she hugged my mother's head close to her chest. Both of them wept silently. Their chests heaving. I felt sorry for my mother's helplessness. I ran to her. She took me in her lap and suddenly she calmed down. She rocked me back and forth on her lap.

'I will never leave you, mommy. I will never leave this house,' I mewed. My mother patted my head softly. I had made up my mind, that I would never leave my mother and my home but my mother had left me and my home. That home ceased to be a home without her.'

Sukhbir could feel her pain today. It was always there but he could never feel it until today. That evening when the Director-General of Police came to meet her, she sat in a garden chair on the back lawn of her bungalow. The lawn was carpeted with velvety green grass. No one was allowed in the garden unless she called. She

MADAM MOHINI - A Romantic Tale of Violence

sat sluggishly and looked around aimlessly. She gave a bored glance at the sky. It was around 4:30 pm but the sun was still shining brightly.

The sky was immaculately blue but full of emptiness. It was quiet to the extent of being dumb. Everything around conspired for the end of winter and marked the onset of spring. The blinding brightness hurt her eyes. Potted ferns on the left of her chair were swaying sleepily with the breeze. Palms did not even look up at the dumb sky, their heads seemed to be moaning. Sukhbir was casually observing all that.

She glanced at the maidservant named Shiela, who was stumping to and fro between a tub of washed clothes and the clothesline, pegging out a series of clothes. Beyond the clothesline stood three papaya trees. Their heads were raised high over the fence. Their leaves were in a noisy argument with the wind. Their fruits hung like the sagging breasts of an old woman which neither carry milk nor can seduce a man.

Sukhbir was busy scribbling something in his diary while she was lost in her thoughts. A junk dealer bellowed in the street. His heavy throaty voice fell like a bombshell and startled her to the bone.

'Fucking bastard...' she murmured almost instantly. 'He is a junk himself...'

Sukhbir heard the thumping of approaching footsteps. Then the thumping changed into a soft rustle because the footsteps were now on the grass. She glanced over

MADAM MOHINI - A Romantic Tale of Violence

her shoulder. It was the Director-General of Police. She roused herself a little.

'Please come,' she said pointing to the chair placed in front of where she was sitting. He was a tall solid man in uniform. Despite the hugeness of his body, there was a remarkable grace in his movement. He thanked her charmingly and sat in the chair. She looked at his heavy face. His smile roused hope in her. She knew intuitively that it was happening at last. The expected message had come. All her life, it seemed, she had been waiting for this to happen. A faint smile appeared on her face. But as soon as it appeared on her face, it vanished from his face. He looked solemn. He was sitting very straight in his chair, his powerful chest swelling and quivering. His face bent down.

Her heart was racing. She was waiting anxiously for him to speak.

'Madam,' he started saying something but paused for a moment as though to choose the appropriate words and began again, 'I...I regret I have got all the records checked but...' he spoke haltingly.

She felt an ache in her chest.

'But no arrest of any woman by the name of your mother was made during those months.' He finally blurted out at one go.

Her heart pounded violently. She was too shocked to say or feel anything. Thoughts stopped occurring as if her mind had blanked out. Her face turned livid.

MADAM MOHINI - A Romantic Tale of Violence

Confusion and terror gripped her. At that moment, Sukhbir couldn't feel the pain that gripped every muscle of her body. She found herself struggling to get her breath back. She knew this terrible agonising pain had always been there but it could not be suffered.

Suddenly she felt the futility of everything around her. Darkness engulfed her from inside and outside. The darkness, even darker than the night her mother had disappeared, even darker than the nights of terror in 1984. It was absolute darkness. She felt that she was sitting in a dungeon with the walls closing upon her. Air was being sucked out as she saw a thin streak of light coming in through one of those dark walls. There was a tiny aperture, as tiny as the tip of a pin. The light filled her eyes and she opened them with a jerk.

The DGP was sitting motionlessly. Neither of them spoke for the next five minutes. As she slowly started breathing easily, some thoughts, though disconnected, started coming to her. At last, she spoke.

'Where could she have gone then? I saw the police taking her away,' her voice was tattered.

'If she is alive, we will find her.' The DGP assured her.

She interrupted him furiously, 'Of course, she is.' With a huge effort she swallowed the lump in her throat.

'Yes, Madam. Since you and I are part of the same system, I would prefer to share my fears with you.' The DGP said confidently.

✦ 173 ✦

MADAM MOHINI - A Romantic Tale of Violence

She looked into his eyes and said nothing. He took it as a signal of her willingness to listen and continued, 'Madam, in those days the police, as I know, cremated thousands of bodies after declaring them unidentified,' he paused for a while and looked a little grim. 'Whenever they get a chance, human beings love to revive the animal inside them. And those times were perfect for a large number of people to do just that. I hope your mother had not become a victim of that.'

She convulsed. 'Mr. Singh,' she breathed deeply, 'I am telling you that she is alive, very much alive. You have to just find her. Understand your duty and perform it,' she spoke firmly.

'Yes, Madam,' he said and saluted her, 'May I take your leave, Madam? I will keep you informed.'

She nodded her head. He left. She kept sitting in her chair, still and frozen. After half an hour, she rose to her feet and limped to her room.

* * * * * * *

'Many years after my mom disappeared, I couldn't think of love dissociated from her. The emotion of love was completely merged with my mother until I met Amrit. I didn't actually realise when love let off a branch that gradually grew into a full-bloom tree. Mynas and cuckoos nestled in that tree. It got laden with the juiciest berries as it matured. Its dense cool shade gave

MADAM MOHINI - A Romantic Tale of Violence

much relief from the scorching sun. The branches laden with lush green leaves and fiery red berries started growing longer and touched the ground. I pushed the overlapping branches aside and crouched through the narrow opening. Inside was a natural alcove, high enough for a man to stand. The sun flashed through the thick network of leaves. Under the tree, the ground was misty with fallen leaves. From somewhere, deeper in the branches, came the droning of an unknown bird.

I thought I was there a bit early. But there were no difficulties there. I would sit and start collecting the fallen berries and smell their sweet scent. A sound at my back would soothe me, the sound of a foot on the twigs. A hand would fall lightly on my shoulder. I would look up and it would be Amrit.

The sweetness of the air and the greenness of the leaves always daunted me. I was comfortable in the knowledge that no one other than him and I knew the existence of that tree and the alcove under it.

Pammi was dead against my studying for the next class. She decided that I would not study further and declared it sternly to Gursimran. He had neither the time nor the patience to argue with his quarrelsome wife. One evening when he happened to cross me in the corridor, he stopped me.

'See, Jeetu's mother doesn't want you to study further. So, it is better that you concentrate on the household chores,' he told me plainly.

MADAM MOHINI - A Romantic Tale of Violence

It came so abruptly that I didn't know how to react. I heard what he said but my mind was too numb to process it. I stood completely still, watching him walk away. After a few steps, he stopped and turned, 'If you dare to carry on, you can try but as you know, it is next to impossible to do anything in this house which she does not will'.

But Amrit was a hardcore optimist and he encouraged me to carry on. I was convinced to such an extent that I started thinking – I can do it. And I actually started squeezing every minute out of my routine and keeping it aside for my studies. Strangely, Pammi began to require my services much more than in the previous years. She was at her best in keeping me on my toes. I was seen running around the house for most of the day.

She would sprawl on her bed and ask me to bring a glass of water. When I brought it, she found it was too cold to drink. 'Bring normal water,' she would shout. I would run back to the kitchen and bring another glass. She would sip it and spit it on my shirt, 'Mad girl, this is too hot, change it'. I would run back again and bring another glass. I extended it to her, my hands trembling. She would look at me sternly and move her hand to hold the glass and before I could realise her intentions, she would deliberately let the glass slip through her hand. The glass would shatter to pieces. Nervous sweat trickled down my temples as I looked at the broken pieces.

MADAM MOHINI - A Romantic Tale of Violence

'What are you staring at now,' she would scream. Her razor-sharp voice shook me, 'Clean it, stupid.' Her eyes flashed as she would mouth silent abuses at me.

Such incidents were routine. She made me stand outside her washroom when she took bath for an hour. She made me dust her room five times a day. She made me hunt down every mosquito in her room. She deliberately kept her bedroom door open in the evening to let the mosquitoes in and laughed vampishly when I ran after them.

Gursimran was right. It was almost impossible to do what she did not want. Despite all that I tried. Other than the external hurdles, there were internal hurdles too. Amrit was not there to teach me and my mind was fast losing the power to concentrate on the books. Even worse was the need to conceal my emotions. Without any warning, he would come to my mind and with it an intolerable desire to be alone. Until I was alone, it was impossible to plan the fine precautionary details about our next meeting. Every moment was engaged in solving the physical problem of how and where to meet Amrit.

I thought of him as I lay awake in bed. I thought of the velvet softness of his lips. It can't be wrong if it feels so right.

After searching for many days, he chose a place for our meetings. It rid me of the everyday mental exercise of thinking of newer and obscurer places which should

✦ 177 ✦

MADAM MOHINI - A Romantic Tale of Violence

also not be far. Presumably, he could be trusted to find a safe place. He informed me of this place through a letter which he threw on the back lawn near the fence. When verbal communication became impossible and many days passed and we were unable to meet, I kept an eye near the fence in wait for his letter. I had to meet him after dinner that day.

The sun disappeared in a boil of red and the chirruping of the evening crickets filled the air. Everyone in the house was fed. Pammi bolted her bedroom door from inside. After a while, the scent of rose wafted through her bedroom window. That was a good sign. It meant she was preparing to busy herself in bed. Jeetu's room was also closed. The rest of the rooms were empty and the kitchen was deserted after being closed for the night.

I skirted the kitchen, cut unseen through the back lawn, and slipped out of the back door. In a minute, I came onto the path Amrit had told me about, a mere cattle track between the bushes on the roadside. A sound at my back froze me, but I continued moving. It was the best thing to do. It might be Amrit or I might have been followed. To look around was to make your guilt obvious. A hand touched my shoulder and I turned. My heart raced. Ah! To my relief it was Amrit. He parted the bushes and quickly led the way along a narrow track to the woods. I followed silently.

The night rolled into the trees. Beetles droned all around. We hopped over a fallen tree and reached a

MADAM MOHINI - A Romantic Tale of Violence

natural clearing surrounded by bushes on all sides and completely shut from the outside world.

'Here we are,' he looked at me and asked in a whisper, 'Do you like it?'

I nodded and without another word took him in my hug. We sat close to each other and made long conversations. We talked about anything we could think of.

Then onwards, our meetings were invariably at night. Over time, it started becoming harder and harder to leave the house like that. I had a feeling that someone in the house doubted me.

In the beginning, our relationship was chaste, going by the definition provided by the traditionalists. Amrit's sense of honour prevented him from doing anything more than pressing his soft lips against my hands or cheeks. But gradually it changed. The prolonged separation, the heartache caused to him because of my inability to keep dates, and an overpowering need for each other created desperation. And soon, I was not sure if it was his skin that I felt or my own. My unbridled response set him aflame and took both of us higher and higher to the unbearable summits of ecstasy. Sometimes we grew reckless and stayed longer, holding on to each other, acutely aware of the minutes ticking away. We stole deep kisses before parting. When we moved apart, both of us sighed deeply.

My feeling that someone in the house knew about my escapades grew stronger by the day. Every time I

MADAM MOHINI - A Romantic Tale of Violence

sneaked out, I felt as if a pair of eyes was boring in my back. I started feeling uneasy.

Once when the gatekeeper passed me in the corridor, he gave a quick sidelong glance that seemed to pierce right into my chest and filled me with horror. I thought he was the one who was spying on me. A close observation for a week made me change my view to some extent. He seemed harmless though I continued feeling a peculiar uneasiness whenever he was near me.

The pale and bent washerman had come to occupy one of the four rooms in one corner of the back lawn. These rooms had been specially designed for servants — dingy and small. Along with him came his wife Sheila and their four children. Pammi let him stay there with his family on the condition that his wife would work in the house for free. Sheila was a colourless crushed looking woman with wispy hair and a wrinkled face. She was a woman of about forty but looked much older. She was always stinking of raw eggs and shit. Her job was to clean the toilets and dump the garbage anywhere out of the house. She carried garbage in an iron basin on her head and dumped it in a vacant plot in the neighbourhood. She had been casting apprehensive glances at me for a few days.

One evening when I was picking up the used teacups left on the grass in the lawn by Pammi, Sheila came dragging her son out of the doorway. The boy was screaming. As soon as she could bring him out, he freed

MADAM MOHINI - A Romantic Tale of Violence

himself from her grip and bolted back inside, and closed the door. I was watching all this with disgust. She looked at me while rubbing her neck. Her eyes flitted from me to the back door twice and then a brutal smile appeared on her lips. Instantly, a chilling wave of terror flowed through me. I got goosebumps. I was almost sure, at least for that moment that she was the one but that idea also couldn't take a vivid shape.

As the days went by, I felt that everyone in that house seemed to be spying on me. I was not sure any longer. A flash of an eye stirred fear and the next flash of the same eye pacified it. The only 'creature' I was able to trust was Bahadur uncle. He often asked me about the progress of my studies. I always managed to dodge his question and continued with my night time adventures. But with a difference. Now a greater part of the original recklessness was replaced by caution. This led to a decline in the frequency of our meetings.

In the beginning, when I expressed my inability to see him so often, he got angry. I felt that I had become a physical necessity for him, something that he not only wanted but felt he had a right to. But over the months, the nature of his desire for me changed. Now, when I held his hand and squeezed it, I seemed to invite affection and not desire. A deep tenderness would suddenly take hold of him. I wished we could walk openly through the streets, without fear. I wished we had a house where we could live together happily.

✦ 181 ✦

MADAM MOHINI - A Romantic Tale of Violence

One night, when I reached the woods, I found him waiting impatiently. I started to hug him but he disengaged himself.

'One second,' he said, 'let me show you what I have brought for you. Look here!' He took out a chocolate from his pocket and opened the wrapper. A sweet smell filled my nostrils. I often smelt it when Jeetu ate it but had tasted it a long time back when my mom had bought it for me. I felt excited.

'How did you get it?' I asked.

'I saved money for this,' he murmured.

I gazed astonishingly at the chocolate and sat down hurriedly to eat it. Both of us relished every bit of it. The taste of that chocolate is still fresh on my tongue.

I often thought about the risk I was taking in meeting him clandestinely. It was almost a folly. My absence from the house could not be concealed forever. If someone came to know, I was sure to be thrown out. We were sitting side-by-side on the dusty ground. I felt his shoulders give a wriggle of dissent. He always contradicted me when I expressed my fears.

'You have somewhere to go,' he said prosaically, 'I will take you with me.'

'Where?' I asked him.

'We will have a house.' He answered in a matter-of-fact way.

'But when?' I questioned him.

MADAM MOHINI - A Romantic Tale of Violence

He fell silent for a while. In a way, he realised that he himself was also doomed. He also knew that sooner or later they will be caught. But another part of his mind believed that they could elope and he would start earning enough to support a wife.

'We will do it. Give me another year. I will not starve you,' he said confidently.

At least I was getting three full meals a day to eat. He was not as fortunate as I was. Sometimes he didn't get anything to eat for a whole day. I pressed myself against him to reassure him with the warmth of my body. A silent promise flowed between us. He squeezed me in his arms to show his gratitude.

I became aware of the silence. He had been very still for some time. I was lying on his side with my cheek pillowed in his hand. My breast rose and fell slowly and regularly. I opened my eyes with the sense of having slept for a long time, but a glance at the sky through the branches told me that it was almost an hour past midnight. I lay dozing for a while then stirred to get up. He held my waist encircling with his arm.

Suddenly, there was a sound, the unmistakable sound of crackling of twigs under feet. We sprang apart. My entrails turned cold. His pupils dilated and his face turned yellow with fear. We could do nothing except stand gazing into each other's eyes. We both were rooted to our spots. There was a snap as though a branch had been broken and then a rustle

✦ 183 ✦

MADAM MOHINI - A Romantic Tale of Violence

coming closer with every second. Our bodies were shaking. There was a stampede of shoes and soon they were there, right in front of us, Gursimran and the gatekeeper.

I received a violent kick on my ankle which flung me to the ground. Then a fist smashed in my belly. I doubled up with pain and gasped for breath. Amrit stood dead still with shock. When his pale face came within the angle of my vision, I saw that he could feel my pain in his body. They dragged me out of the alcove and for an instant, our eyes met, I bade him a silent goodbye.

Gursimran pushed me violently. I fell almost flat on my face. A sharp cry of pain wrung out of me. I raised my head slightly. Pammi stood there with her eyes exuding fire and her nostrils flaring like those of a buffalo. Her eyes were fixed on me as if a hungry hyena was getting ready to eat a sumptuous meal.

'Throw her out. This house is not for bloody whores,' she shouted at her husband.

'Let her be hungry for some days. The ghost of love will fly out of her head,' shouted Gursimran.

'I have declared,' she wagged her finger at me, 'that I will not see her defiled body in this house.'

My heart was thumping with frightening loudness. I stayed still on the floor as there was nothing that I could do. I watched them walking out and bolting my room from outside.

MADAM MOHINI - A Romantic Tale of Violence

Against my fears, they didn't throw me out of their house. I was relieved and felt deeply obliged to them till I came to know why I was not thrown out?

* * * * * * *

Chapter 8

'A year later...
The days were burning hot. Only two weeks of canvassing were left. The preparations were in full swing and all members of the house along with hundreds of Gursimran's associates were working overtime. Gursimran was a candidate for the legislative assembly from Patiala. By giving him a ticket, the CM had amply rewarded him for his loyalties of the past as well as the present. Now it was only his effort that could fetch him a win. Processions, rallies, meetings everything was being organised. Voters were being influenced, cajoled, pampered, and bought. Thousands of posters were pasted all over the city – anywhere and everywhere – from dustbins to poles of street lights, from lavatory walls to pavements. Slogans were coined and rumours about the opponents were floated. Pamphlets were distributed. Nothing was being left to chance and no effort was being spared.

In addition to my regular work, I spent hours preparing tea and snacks for the workers who thronged

MADAM MOHINI - A Romantic Tale of Violence

the house daily. Bahadur uncle was equally busy, in fact, more than me as he also had to make frequent errands to the market to fetch one grocery item or the other. Every hour we discovered that something or the other had gone out of stock and was immediately needed.

Gursimran went from village to village till the late hours of the night, serving the villagers with cheap country liquor. People danced savagely with the beating of the drums. The whole length and breadth of his constituency was immersed in a grand party. The party helped Gursimran to raise a squad of volunteers who was busy day and night stitching banners, painting posters, and erecting flags. Gursimran's days were fuller than ever. Though he was overworked, he looked as happy as a lark. He was everywhere at once waving, shouting slogans, pushing, and pulling. Money was being spent like water. Payments to liquor shops, meat shops, sweetmeat shops, tent houses, and many more, were made every day and sometimes even twice a day. Pammi liked only the one-way flow of money that is inwards. She hated the outward flow. She was seen arguing with her husband, 'What if you didn't win?'

'Must your black tongue wag?' Gursimran got furious.

'I mean, at least save some money,' Pammi argued.

'Stupid woman, think of it... What if we win, we will earn thousand times of what we would have spent,' he raised his voice to make sure that it entered her head.

MADAM MOHINI - A Romantic Tale of Violence

'We have collected a lot of money in the last few years. You have squandered enough of it. What else can we do with it if we keep it? This is the ultimate investment, the ultimate business.'

'But a big risk too,' she uttered impatiently.

'I am quite ready to take it. This time it is only money. You were not so hopeless or worried when I risked my life for it,' Gursimran's comment sounded bitter. Pammi flinched for a second and then quickly said, 'I am with you dear,' her voice was extremely polite, 'go ahead'.

The enormity of the extent fascinated me in the beginning. Soon I started getting bored of that atmosphere of sizzling enthusiasm. Everything was physical and external to me. I never paid a thought to the consequences because I believed that they won't change anything in and around me. I would continue to be a servant either way.

It was the last day of the campaign. A huge rally had been organised in the heart of the city. Gursimran decided to take Jeetu along and for his care, I was the most suited, even more than Pammi, so I was taken along. The venue was packed with several thousand people. Gursimran stood with his coterie on a green carpeted platform. He gripped the neck of the microphone with one hand and the other moved violently in the air. His voice was made metallic by loudspeakers.

He started his speech with promises. After a few minutes, he started attacking the opposition and that

MADAM MOHINI - A Romantic Tale of Violence

made his speech endless. At every few moments, the sentiments of the crowd boiled over and his voice would get drowned by the wild roaring of slogans by the crowd. The speech had been going on for half an hour and was likely to continue for another hour or two. I started feeling bored. It was impossible to listen any longer to him and the savage yells of the crowd.

I glanced at Jeetu who was sitting beside me. He was fully engrossed and fascinated in watching his father howling into the microphone. He was quite excited. I guessed he was not likely to get any respite from this enthusiasm very soon. I tapped his shoulder and gave him a stern look, 'Don't move from here till I am back,' I said aloud.

He gave a blank expression which showed he couldn't hear. The sounds around seemed invincible. I tried louder, this time taking my mouth almost inside his ear. He nodded timidly. I pushed my way through the crowd. I walked fast so as to get out of the range of the yelling sounds of the rally. I was feeling excited as I was out of the house after almost a year. The last time was when I had gone on my own but had been brutally dragged back. After that, I had firmly made up my mind not to place myself at any kind of risk. Though Amrit's face floated in and out of my memory, I was too busy to think of him for any long duration of time. Sometimes when my yearning to see him became acute, I asked Bahadur uncle after Amrit.

❖ 189 ❖

MADAM MOHINI - A Romantic Tale of Violence

'Was all well with him?' I would ask.

'I don't know,' he would reply disinterestedly.

'Will you find out,' I would request feebly.

'No,' he would reply coldly. Gradually, I stopped asking.

Now, I was in a narrow bazaar adjacent to the rally venue. It was a narrow, metalled road with shops on either side. There were also little stalls that sold street food, coloured nadas (trouser strings) and *parandis* (braid strings), cheap cosmetics, and hair clips. I strolled past a *jutti* shop which was full of bright and shimmering *juttis* (footwear). They were available in all colours and sizes, handcrafted out of leather and decorated with coloured clothes and beads.

I remembered one such pair which my mommy owned. She had got it made in Jagraon from a famous cobbler, matching it with her wedding dress. It was covered with the same red silk fabric from which her dress was made. It had golden beaded fringes and a small bunch of tiny golden bells at its pointed front. I looked at them with awe and she would smile and let me wear them. My feet filled only half of them. I would run around the house listening to the jingling sound made by the tiny bells. I tripped now and then but never took them off unless I was asked to do so by mommy with an amused smile and a promise that she would buy me many such or even more beautiful ones when I grew up. For a moment forlornness descended upon me like a shroud.

MADAM MOHINI - A Romantic Tale of Violence

I moved on. I strolled past shops — sweet shops, flower shops, shops that sold suits for women and men. There were the tailors' shops. I saw men and women sewing buttons, hemming women's shirts, and ironing clothes. Embroiders were busy intricating coloured threads over the traced patterns on the fabrics. I watched the fat bored-looking shopkeepers in their big shops. Out of curiosity, I peeked into a phulkari seller's shop. Thousands of phulkaris were stacked on the wooden racks behind the counter. The salesmen were busy rolling out bright coloured phulkaris to their customers who were mostly women. One of the salesmen looked at me, scanned me from top to bottom. He instantly judged that I was not a potential customer and blatantly ignored me. I felt slightly embarrassed.

I moved further down the road and walked among a steady stream of pedestrians, rickshaws, and bicycle riders. People were constantly moving in and out of the shops. I reached the Lord Shiva's temple, sandwiched between two shops, and for a while, stood in front of it. Its tower was made of red sandstone and carved with intricate figures of the numerous gods and goddesses we have in our country. The steps which led to the temple door were flanked by two glossy white marble statues of holy cows supposedly sitting in the 'on-guard' position. I ran my fingers on one of them. It felt amazingly smooth. I looked at its face. It gazed back at me with its opaque white eyes.

MADAM MOHINI - A Romantic Tale of Violence

The temple had a wide flight of stairs that buffered the temple from the road. The altar was visible through the open door. I could see a saffron *dhoti* (groin cloth) clad priest busy playing mediator between the devotees and Lord Shiva. I had a glimpse of a bent woman handing over a packet of offerings to the priest and the latter urging Shiva to accept them. Then he kept the packet aside, applied a sandal tilak on her forehead, and gave her some *parsad*. The woman turned to go. The priest surveyed the contents of the bag of offerings. He seemed to be assessing what items were to be sold at the outside *parsad* shop for recycling. He might have had some other thoughts also but since I only had his rear view it didn't convey more.

After some more wandering, I decided to go back before Jeetu raised a hue and cry, making my absence conspicuous. While going back, I couldn't help myself from stopping in front of the display window of a small Phulkari shop to do a last-minute marvelling at their designs and colours. I stood there for a while mystified at how they created those and at the fineness of their silks. They made me aware of my own lowliness, my plain looks, my inability to think of ever buying these marvels.

Suddenly, someone tapped me on my shoulder. I turned. My pulse fluttered. A sound, something between a squeak and a gasp escaped my lips. I felt giddy with excitement and fear. Amrit was there in front of me with the same companionable smile donning his face.

MADAM MOHINI - A Romantic Tale of Violence

My mouth gaped but before I could say a word, he 'shushed' me and motioned me to follow him. He led me inside the same phulkari shop. The shop owner was not at the counter and neither were there any customers. Another young man with deep-set brooding eyes was smiling at me.

'Please cover for me and watch for the master,' Amrit requested that man.

'Don't worry brother,' the young man smiled pleasantly.

He took me to the store at the rear end of the shop. It had piles of packed and yet-to-be-packed phulkaris. Then he looked at my face and pulled me to him and held me for a long, long time. His chest was heaving. I could feel the soothing warmth oozing out of every pore of his body and entering the mine. When he finally released me, I could see that he was crying.

'I missed you so much,' his voice quavered.

'Me too,' I wondered at the characteristic ritualism in my voice. I didn't know why my words were just hollow sounds. They seemed to be lacking any feeling.

'Are you working here?' I asked.

'Yes.' He replied with a smile.

'Studies?' I questioned him.

'No, I left. I have to make money so that I can marry you,' he said broadening his chest.

An involuntary smile appeared on my lips. I could feel myself blushing. I felt it coming back — the excitement,

✦ 193 ✦

MADAM MOHINI - A Romantic Tale of Violence

the emotions, the pride — all in a big giant wave that filled my being. Something in him, in his smile and his broad protective chest, pulled me and I drew closer to him and rested my cheek on his chest. We stood that way for a short while.

'I will save for our home. Then we will open a small shop...,' he thought for a moment. 'A book shop, just a little place enough for us to earn a living and we would read them too, newer and newer every time,' he said dreamily. Then he grew quiet. We were brow to brow. I felt the heat of his breath on my lips. I wondered at the softness of his lips, at the feel of his hands on my neck.

Suddenly, I remembered that I had to go. I jumped aside.

'I have to go,' my voice was beginning to panic. His chin trembled. I made my way out of the shop. I sensed a shift in the atmosphere. I felt all eyes looking at me. I heard whispers. My hands began to sweat. I imagined that they all knew what I had done in there, that they would go and blurt it to Pammi. I dabbed the sweat on my forehead with the fringe of my *dupatta* and then clutching my *dupatta* close to my chest I pushed through the crowd.

I ran and ran until I reached the venue. Panic slowly vaporised and my breath started slowing down. Gursimran was still howling into the microphone. People were still yelling but with lesser enthusiasm. Jeetu was where I had left him. A few minutes later, I looked back expecting to see exactly what I saw. Amrit was there beyond a moving crowd of people, half-hidden by the corner of a shop. He gave me a wounded look.

That night, I kept getting distracted in the kitchen. I was not able to concentrate on anything. The *rotis* were not round and they kept getting burnt.

'Your roti is burning,' Bahadur uncle would tell. He was serving them and every time a burnt roti was served, Pammi shouted at him. But all I could think of was the fullness of Amrit's lips, the heat of his breath on my cheeks, his passionate kisses and the way I melted in his hug. The peculiar smell of new cloth which had filled that shop came back to me.

'*Roti* is burning,' said Bahadur, this time a little louder and irritated, 'Where are you?'

'Sorry. I am... I don't know.' I stammered.

Bahadur nodded uncertainly. His gaze lingered on me.

I was unable to sleep that night and kept rolling from side to side. I tried to remember all those things which I had made myself forget with continuous efforts. The blunted edges of old memories started scratching my mind. A loss I had stopped wailing about, came back to me, again. The pain of being away from him, the sharp pain of a fist smashing in my belly, the bumping of my frightened heart, the pain of being called a whore, and the shame and the guilt. And beyond all that the astonishing ease with which we both had got into each

MADAM MOHINI - A Romantic Tale of Violence

other, the spontaneity of it. Amidst all that loneliness and ugliness, what I did was not a sin unforgivable. In fact, it was not a sin at all.

All thoughts of promiscuity and reputation seemed absurd and the sweet scent of berries came back, the light filtering through the thick network of branches and the leaves fallen on the moist ground under it. It all came back. I saw myself in the alcove sitting beside Amrit, the air thick with passion. A conviction started taking shape in my mind. I started thinking that what Amrit and I did was not sinful, it was natural and beautiful. Then the planning started in my mind — I should go to him, run away from this wretchedness, and be embraced by love. Cradled by these beautiful thoughts of a romantic life, I finally slipped into sleep, sound and sweet.

In my dream, I saw my mommy. She was sitting up in bed with a red bedsheet. The bed was under a dense mulberry tree with lush leaves and purple berries. I was busy picking the berries that came pouring down with every gust of wind while she was sewing buttons on my frock. Then I heard her sob, a real sorrow-drenched sob. 'What happened mommy?' I took her lovely face in my tiny hands. She pointed towards a man who was going away. When he stopped and turned back, I saw his face. He was Akashdeep.

'He is leaving. He is actually leaving,' she said in a choked voice and pulled me closer to her chest. I clung to her.

MADAM MOHINI - A Romantic Tale of Violence

'Maybe it is senseless to want to be with someone when bullets are raining and blood is flowing through the streets,' her voice was as low as a whisper.

* * * * * * *

After all the activity-packed days, there was unprecedented jubilation in the house. Every mouth was ripping with a wide smile. It was a hot muggy afternoon. The bone-scratching heat stifled the air like smoke. I was working in the kitchen sweating through my kameez. Every exhaled breath caused a burning sensation in my nose. I was aware of the celebrations which were to take place in the evening. I heard voices around. Jeetu's exhilarated shrieks and Pammi talking on the phone to the whole world. The phone had been ringing non-stop since the morning and Pammi attended all the calls with undying eagerness. Her voice was swollen with the pride of a queen. My heart was gripped with apprehensions wondering how her behaviour would change after this event? How would she take Gursimran's victory to her hollow head? And how, most importantly, things would change for me?

* * * * * * *

A catering team was busy on the front lawn. It was lined with foldable tables along the wall. The tables were then covered with white cotton sheets with pink

MADAM MOHINI - A Romantic Tale of Violence

satin frills. Many round tables with chairs around them were being arranged on the lawn. Some men were busy fixing stringed lights on the walls and on the eves of the roof. Though the evening was hot and hardly fit for a party yet the occasion was so profound that a party was inevitable. In the evening, people started pouring in. I sat in one corner with my hands between my knees watching all that was taking place. Though there was nothing much for me to do but I had to be at the beck and call of the masters. They could call me anytime for anything. Many men gave congratulatory hugs to Gursimran. Many just shook hands with constipated smiles. Some simply folded their hands diplomatically with a slightly bent head. Women hugged and patted Pammi, who was on top of the world.

With every such pat and hug, her chest broadened and her bulky boobs popped out. She was vainly trying to cover their hugeness under her dupatta. That day, for some reason, which I deciphered later, she had covered her head too. From that day onwards she always did so, especially when some politically important people were around or when she went out in public. That way she looked very docile and quite a Sikh. Later, she also bought some new strings of pearls to wear around her neck.

The men sat on the white upholstered chairs around the tables. They drank the expensive scotch that was being served and ate the specially cooked snacks. They spoke in bantering tones about Gursimran's dazzling

MADAM MOHINI - A Romantic Tale of Violence

victory and overall, of the party. They talked about the upcoming government and their personal businesses and political plans for the forthcoming five years.

'This is how it works; you scratch my back I scratch yours,' one tall lanky young Sikh was saying while chewing on a meatball and everyone laughed aloud.

From the excited voices and the snippets of conversation that I caught I put together what was happening. Gursimran had won the elections and he was also getting a berth in the cabinet. The Ministry of Education had already been promised to him. Though his friends didn't consider it a very lucrative one, Gursimran was happy. Once he entered the cabinet he would plan further. Our now CM was to be the CM at that time. He has an assured way of rewarding his people.

The air was thick with the smell of sizzling lamb, roasted chicken, and basmati rice. In one corner two cooks were busy fanning fire under the grill on which the chicken legs were roasting. Gursimran and one of his close confidants, who was often seen in the house, were discussing something important. Their faces were scrunched up in concentration. Jeetu was shuffling around the snack tables tasting one snack after another. After stuffing his mouth, he would stand near a group of adults and listen to their talk while chewing over the stuffing in his mouth.

* * * * * * *

✦ 199 ✦

MADAM MOHINI - A Romantic Tale of Violence

Bahadur uncle gestured me to come and eat. I hesitated and looked around. Pammi was busy chatting with a bunch of women. I worked up the nerve and started filling my plate with all the delicacies till it was a huge pile and my plate refused to accommodate anymore. I sat in a corner and started eating. It was delicious. I had never eaten such food that too in plenty. On occasions my father used to bring home some chicken, it was never enough for overeating. My mother rationed out my share. If I needed more, I had to eat out of my mother's share which she readily gave. I was never supposed to take a morsel from my father's share.

* * * * * * *

Thereafter, things changed fast. Gursimran opened up an office at home along with the one that he had somewhere outside. He became serious, talking with a newly attained composure. He was very careful while speaking, only counted and well-weighted words came out of him now. He resorted to wearing only white *kurta pajamas* and navy-blue turban. He stopped colouring his beard which turned milky white making him look at least ten years older. He regularly started visiting Gurudwaras and tried to make a show of it whenever possible. He had bought himself a new *kirpan (sword)* and a sword belt and wore it proudly across his chest. His smile grew plastic and gave an illusion

✦ 200 ✦

MADAM MOHINI - A Romantic Tale of Violence

of benevolence. He walked past people who gathered almost daily to meet him, with a rare nimbleness. This made him look perpetually busy. He earnestly devoted himself to amassing wealth. In short, he became very, very busy.

Pammi, on the other hand, no longer had that perpetual severe scowl on her brow. She smiled openly and more frequently. She started dressing up in shades of pastels and whites with matching silk dupattas to cover her head and breasts. She wore only pearls and diamonds, pearls when she went to inaugurate schools, orphanages, or old age homes or funerals and diamonds were for tea parties which she often threw for the wives of the high-ups of the city or when she was invited to any such party.

In public her smile was tight-lipped. She pretended total concentration while listening to the business presentations that people made. She became an expert at nodding her head at the right instances making the other person feel that she understood every bit of the subject under consideration. She hired an educated young man to write her speeches. Eventually, she also converted one of the rooms in the house into her office.

I remember how one morning she ate her breakfast hastily. She hurriedly shovelled the last bite of her fourth *aloo parantha* into her fat mouth. She covered her mouth and burped and then quickly left the table for her office.

✦ 201 ✦

MADAM MOHINI - A Romantic Tale of Violence

'Come with me, count the number of people and bring tea for everyone,' she hurled the order to me.

There were four people, all men. They wanted to open an academy for which Gursimran's favour was required. Pammi listened to them with real concentration this time. She was trying to hide her interest in getting the project passed and it made her face distorted in a new and strange way. Later that day, I overheard her arguing with her husband. I tiptoed to the door. Pammi was pressing her point to him. The arguments were in low-pitched voices.

'I can't allow this.' Gursimran said calmly.

'But why? What is wrong? They are offering enough.' She said impatiently.

'Not enough.' He replied determinedly.

'It is enough.' She reiterated.

Finally, after a lot of debate, he relented. It set me thinking about how Pammi could settle down for a lesser gain. It was later that I comprehended her farsightedness when more and more people started pushing their files through her. With every success, she gained importance among people. Every argument that she took up with Gursimran settled in her favour and she walked out of the room, triumphant, smirking inwardly. In short, she was even busier.

* * * * * * *

MADAM MOHINI - A Romantic Tale of Violence

As the darkness soaked the sunlight from the sky, I was lying still in my bed. Absently I touched the new necklace I had made out of green peas. I felt the hardness they had acquired after drying up. Two nights ago, and again last night, I had woken up mid-sleep. I was torn between two situations — to stay or not to stay. Should I continue being a servant here or should I go to Amrit and be a master. I met him only once since that rally day. How hard it had been to plan and materialise that meeting! But it brought tremendous satisfaction and made all that effort worthwhile.

But in a distant corner of my mind, a question kept nagging me. Was I not making a mistake? The horrors of Delhi darkened my mind. I could feel the shadow of a huge monster over me, rendering everything else invisible. Seasons had come and gone. Terrorists had been defeated and tamed, old battles had ended and new ones; the political ones; had started. But I hardly cared. All this did not affect me. I passed the years in wait - the cruellest wait for my mother. Time stretched when my heart longed for her the most, time contracted when my mind got busy with things that gave even the slightest of pleasures.

Time had been very unkind to me. I hoped there were kinder years still waiting to happen in my life. I was waiting for a new life, a life in which I would be with my mother. Then one day a prince would come riding a white horse, the same way as it happened in fairy tales,

MADAM MOHINI - A Romantic Tale of Violence

and take me with him. But all those happy thoughts were smothered under the shadow of that huge monster. There was just a stony silence, a wan look, a sudden attack of grief, as I again smelt the burning flesh and hair. I heard wails, saw sighing and grieving people in the refugee camp, crowding my room and closing upon me.

Over the years, I had ample occasions to think about how things might have turned out for me if I had not trusted Mani. I would not have spent the night outside her husband's house in the rain. I would not have watched the Delhi sky darken, the shadows engulfing the houses, and fires engulfing the people. I would have stayed at my Nani's house and mommy would surely have come looking for Nani and me.

My neck and back were sore from lying sleeplessly in bed. I sat up and looked out of the window. The crickets chirruped. Overhead, I could see the clouds slide past a pale moon. Dogs barked somewhere. I steadied myself against the waves of dismay passing through me. A gust of wind busted through the window and gently touched my face.

'Mom...' I uttered with a deep sigh and my eyes started watering. I wept and wept and shed all those tears which I had not shed when a fist had smashed in my belly or when I had shuffled about being waylaid or when I felt imbalanced on being separated from Amrit or even when loneliness consumed me absolutely. I had not cried in a long time but that night I cried my heart

MADAM MOHINI - A Romantic Tale of Violence

out. In the end, it seemed some burden had been lifted from my shoulders and the mist cleared. I could think better and more clearly. So I thought, I would rely on Amrit. I pulled up the sheet over my face. I felt relieved after making that decision.

To put my plan into action the first step was to accumulate money. So, I started saving money. Tips had become quite frequent in this house as more and more visitors were coming home. Each one of them gave me ten or twenty or some even fifty rupees for serving them tea and snacks. I saved up almost all of it and kept planning. One morning I was making Gursimran's bed. I shook the bedsheet, and while I watched it settling down on its own that I saw a hundred rupees bill crumpled up near the edge of the mattress. I looked around furtively, fluttered my eyes around, and seeing no one around I picked it up in an instant and pushed it into my bra. That was a lottery.

With prosperity showering on this fortunate household, such lotteries had also become frequent. Another day when my iron was hissing over Gursimran's white kurta, I felt something in its side pocket. I slid my hand in and was thrilled to find ten bills of hundred rupees each. 'Wow,' the word erupted in muffled excitement. In six to seven months, I had collected almost seven thousand rupees.

There was also another telephone in the house now. It excited me more than anybody else. It brought the

MADAM MOHINI - A Romantic Tale of Violence

possibility of Amrit talking to me on the phone. With only one phone, it was almost impossible to even think about speaking to him as whenever that phone rang there was more than one person to attend to it. This new line was to be fixed in Pammi's office so obviously, this line would be free during the nights. It had been months since I had met Amrit. The last time when I met him, I gave him this number and told him never to call before fixing it with me.

That day, while I was drying laundry on the roof, I saw Amrit in the street. He gestured that he would call at 10:00 pm that night. I stealthily crept into Pammi's office before the appointed time. I kept my trembling hand on the receiver. My heart was battering against my ribs and blood thudding in my ears. My mouth was dry with fear and anxiety. Every now and then, I peered through the crack in the window curtains. My mind was warning me that I was unnecessarily committing an absolute folly. I was certain that Pammi would come to know. That any moment she would drag me out of the office and ask me whether I had really taken her for such a bitch that she would not find out...that she would let go every time? At that instant, the phone rang and I leapt at the receiver.

'Hello,' I whispered.

'Hello,' said Amrit quite loudly.

'Hey, listen,' I hushed him.

'Be a little louder. I can't hear,' he got even louder.

'Shhhh... Listen, only urgent talk. Ten thousand bucks, when to plan?' I was talking urgently in short bursts.

We talked in hushed voices for about a minute and in that critical minute, important information was successfully exchanged.

I started an anxious wait for the fixed day which was four months from then, on the fifth day of March. The point behind this decision was that I would be eighteen by then. After that phone conversation, I often found myself seized by bouts of euphoria or attacks of mouth-drying anxiety. I was also often consumed by the most scandalous thoughts of his bare body entangled with mine. Lying in bed at night, I would picture him kissing my belly. I wondered at the feel of his hands on my neck and my chest, my back and lower still. Sometimes thinking this way made me feel guilty but at the same time, I relished that peculiar warm sensation that spread up from my belly to my face and my face would become hot.

* * * * * * *

It was a cold overcast day in January, three months before I turned eighteen. I was folding Jeetu's shirts which I had plucked from the clothesline in the yard. I didn't know how long Bahadur uncle had been standing by the doorway hands cupped around a cup of tea. I

MADAM MOHINI - A Romantic Tale of Violence

turned around and was startled to see him and said, 'What uncle?'

'Tea for you,' he said. He looked a little serious.

'Oh! Thank you. You seem to be brooding,' I said while resuming my work.

'The Master is calling you.' He told me quietly.

'Oh please, you see to it. I would rather finish this work,' I said while I continued my work.

'No dear, you need to come. They want to talk to you,' and he left.

Surprised, I looked at his back and then went over to Pammi's bedroom. They sat across from me, Gursimran and his wife, at the small tea table in their bedroom. Pammi was wearing a flimsy lemon-yellow *dupatta* on her head while he was in his ever-white *Kurta pajama*. She poured water from a bottle into one of the two glasses lying on the table. She put the glass before me. That was a surprise, a gesture that was impossible. It immediately raised alarm bells in my mind and set me thinking. All kinds of apprehensions filled my mind. Was the water poisoned? Why would she want to kill me? Or were they going to ask me to leave? That would rather be good for me. Or was there any bad news for me? No. That couldn't be possible. No! No way.

'Well,' she spoke at last. My mind stopped fleeting.

'I... I mean we want... We have an offer for you.' She started hesitantly.

I caught a quick exchange of glances between them.

MADAM MOHINI - A Romantic Tale of Violence

'We have a marriage proposal for you,' Pammi said more clearly.

My heart fell to my toes.

'What?' my head was going numb.

'Yes, we want you to marry Jeetu,' this time Gursimran spoke. My chest tightened.

'This is not an ordinary offer. We are giving you the place of our daughter, elevating you from a ditch to the throne,' Pammi was saying.

'The ground was shifting beneath my feet. Everything around was spinning like a movie playing in fast-forward mode.

'You would live like a queen! He is a little less intelligent than you but he is a man, after all, and the only heir to this rich empire,' Gursimran went on.

I couldn't keep a record of who said what after that. My head was spinning.

'You have a brilliant offer. Think logically.'

I was staring at the wall beyond them. Then they grew quiet. They were watching me, waiting. A silence floated in the air.

'Say something,' Pammi said.

I was struck blind. I opened my mouth, but all that came out was a single, pained groan.

'Let her decide,' Gursimran said to his wife and then to me, 'Take your time. Think it over.'

I couldn't sleep that night. I lay in bed looking out of the window at the sky, listening to the footsteps outside.

MADAM MOHINI - A Romantic Tale of Violence

Sheets of rain were slapping against the window. I was missing mommy in such a crippling manner that I couldn't feel my limbs. It was freezing even under the quilt. Everything looked drab. I pulled up the quilt to my chin to ward off the chill. I dozed off. I was startled awake by a nightmare in the middle of the night. I heard the sound of drizzle outside my window.

The daylight steadily bleached the darkness from the sky. The morning sun was falling flat on the roof and birds were chirping in the rain-washed green trees. I could hear the house coming to life. Some footsteps across the veranda...a sudden hoot from Jeetu. A car buzzed past in the street. A siren approached and then muted. I lay awake in the bed listening to all these sounds. My eyes ached. Then my room's door creaked open. I raised my head and slowly slid out of my bed. Pammi stood in the doorway, just a massive block of black against the bright sunlight behind her.

'Yes,' I said through my numb lips. I sensed that she smiled. She came closer to me and hugged me, for the first time ever.

'Very good. Wise girl,' she said almost bursting with joy.

* * * * * * *

The marriage was to be a grand affair. Pammi was enormously busy with the preparations. After all, Jeetu was her only son and there were hardly any chances of

MADAM MOHINI - A Romantic Tale of Violence

him getting married. Jewellers, cloth dealers, caterers, and many others were coming home one after the other. The wedding dresses were chosen. I was never consulted about anything. I shuffled around the house the whole day, feeling useless and desperately waiting for the drama to be over. One day, I heard her talking on the phone.

'I am such a lucky woman. I knew I should do something for others now. And you see, charity begins at home. My husband is a true gentleman. He encouraged me to do all this,' she was gushing to someone. So I was being presented as a charity.

The news of the wedding spread fast. After some days while I was staring blankly at the ceiling of my room, I heard the office phone ringing. It was 10:00 pm. No one took the call. It kept on ringing frantically and at last Pammi picked up the receiver, 'Hello.' I heard her irritated sharp voice.

'Hello... Hello...' and then the sound of the receiver being banged. My heart missed a beat. A metal claw gripped my belly. Then a pang of guilt set in. The clock ticked louder and louder. The phone ring sounded in my head, deafeningly loud. Then bleak isolation and murderous loneliness.

'Why did you do this? Why did you accept this?' I imagined Amrit beseeching, pleading with me.

I was thinking of my mother. I would never be able to explain to Amrit how and why this offer meant so much to me. It was a business deal for me. That how

✦ 211 ✦

MADAM MOHINI - A Romantic Tale of Violence

it had given me hope, a bleak one though, yet a hope nonetheless. The hope of getting into a better position to find my mother.

'I am sorry. I had to make a choice.' Then my eyes teared over. My eyes flowed until all was quiet save the chirruping of the night bird, the hoot of a distant train, and my own heart thudding ruefully in my chest.

The phone rang every night. Someone would lift the receiver and utter a monotonous Hello-Hello as if already expecting no answer. I was afraid of that pattern of blank calls becoming obvious to the people at home. At the same time, I had to consciously guard myself against reaching the threshold of any dangerous thoughts of running away, of leaving everything behind. I had already decided not to sacrifice anything at the altar of love. No, that was not to be done. And that is when my self-training started, a training to have control over my own mental processes as complete as a story writer has over her characters.

The phone stopped ringing the night before the wedding. Slowly, the memories of Amrit became different. They stood out in my mind disconnectedly. They were like hazy images. I knew that over time these images would also fade. A day would come when the details of his face will also slip out of my memory. I will not miss him as I did then.'

'MADAM...' Her thoughts were interrupted by Sukhbir. He was visibly perplexed. His body stirred as

MADAM MOHINI - A Romantic Tale of Violence

he remembered that man, a shabby-looking man who had stood beyond the hedge at her rally venue, who had been eliminated at Madam's orders, his name was also Amrit. Sukhbir appeared to be thinking hard. Madam gave an all-knowing nod.

'Was he the same man who stood at the edge of the crowd in the rally that day?' he asked. Madam nodded passively.

'What was the need to eliminate him?' Sukhbir sounded extremely sad.

'The gap between us was unbridgeable. We stood on extremely different pedestals. I perceived him as a threat to my career at that time. So, he had to go. I wasn't making choices. The choices were making me,' she said grimly and came back to the story.

'A week before the wedding, Pammi sent for me. She sat beside a pile of newly stitched bright coloured clothes. She flashed me a smile. I smiled back. I could sense the fakeness of both the smiles. Something was hiding behind both. I was not certain though, about what was behind hers.

'Come and sit,' she said extending her arm to me. 'All these are for you.' She said pointing at the pile of new clothes.

Perhaps, I didn't respond the way she expected. Perhaps, she expected to see a bright gleam of excitement in my eyes. Instead, my eyes bore a lethargic faraway look. I felt a weight on my eyelids and a vague

✦ 213 ✦

MADAM MOHINI - A Romantic Tale of Violence

restlessness in my body. She frowned. She lifted the red wedding dress. It cascaded open onto her lap. It was of bright red silk embroidered with green and golden beads and laced with golden tape.

'How is it?' she asked. The blank expression persisted on my face. She shrugged and tossed the dress brusquely on the bed and shot me a disgusted look. I cringed inwardly. Something in me was telling me that she would not shout at me. That she can't, at least for now. And I was right. She nodded and cleared her throat, 'What? Is there something more that you want?' she asked perfectly politely.

'Yes.' I replied.

'What?' She asked surprised with her eyebrows raised.

'I want to visit my home.' I told her softly.

'O!' she sounded relieved, 'I will tell the driver to take you.'

The next morning, the car entered my village. Two barefooted children chased it till it reached my house. The front iron gate was missing. The plaster had chipped from many places off the front wall exposing the bricks. The walls had turned almost black due to the deposition of moss over the years. Wild grass stubbornly blocked the entrance. I opened the lock. It was jammed by rust. A large fluttering spider web struck my face. I removed its fine silky strands from my skin. It was dim inside. Weeds had sprung up along the fungus-infested walls. Some had

MADAM MOHINI - A Romantic Tale of Violence

even grown halfway up the walls. The pane of the rear window was shattered. I peeped out and saw that the back wall had a big hole in it. The floor of the backyard was covered with dead leaves and empty liquor bottles. Perhaps, some people had been using the house.

I sat down with my back against the wall. A wail was trapped in my throat. There were spider webs all around and the ceiling fans were gone. The TV set had gone. There was nothing left in the kitchen. There was a bird's nest on the curtain bracket. The furniture had all rotted. I closed my eyes and summoned my mother into my eyes. The soft radiance of her face soothed me for a while. I laid my face in her warm lap and she swayed back and forth. I could feel her breath. I could feel her heartbeat. I didn't notice when I started crying.

I opened my eyes and stood up. I walked out of the house. My head was heavy and my body was exhausted. I bolted the door and locked it again. Before I turned away, I took a long look at the house. The driver was surrounded by many people. When he spotted me, he hurried to the driver's seat. I got a glimpse of the faces. They projected a mix of expressions —surprise, shock and amusement.

I remember all too well the inescapable drudgery of those days. How had time dragged me along, bruised me?'

* * * * * * *

Chapter 9

'Two years later, Pammi and I were coming back from one of the gynaecologists. These visits were a regular affair since the wedding. The gynae would do regular tests on Jeetu and me and after some weeks would declare, 'The couple is perfectly normal Madam.' This would start another round of frantic phone calls from Pammi to her gossip buddies. A serious talk would be followed by a visit from one of them. One could make out that Pammi was in distress. I often watched her from a distance. She would cluck her tongue and toss her head in despair. Her friend would gently put a hand on her shoulder and speak some sorrow dripping words of consolation. Pammi even sobbed sometimes.

'Don't worry, I know a doctor,' one of her gossip buddies took off. 'You remember Sarwan?'

Pammi gave a lost look.

'Sarwan, my sister-in-law's friend's daughter,' the buddy looked at her searchingly trying hard to remind her through the reference.

'Oh! Yes,' Pammi uttered sullenly. She was clearly pretending to remember so as to bring the talk to the point.

'She got pregnant after four years or so! She is blessed with a son now.' The buddy slapped her knee.

'How?' Pammi was gaping.

'Doctor Gupta, she is too good.' The buddy told her conspiratorially.

And that is how our next doctor was decided. Each reference of a new doctor filled her with hope. But she was always left grimmer in the end. Her restlessness gave me perverse pleasure. Every time the doctor uttered those five words — *the couple is perfectly normal.* I would smile inwardly. Those words made her either very angry or very sad. I gave a controlled expression of genuine sorrow but inwardly I was thrilled, 'You fathead, you can't make an heir for your wealth unless I want it. You made me suffer, now it is your turn'. She wanted grandchildren and that is why she had made me marry that moron.

Jeetu stood almost a foot taller than me. His face was leaner and bearded. His shoulders were narrow and his upper body slumped whenever he saw me. He tied his hair at the back of his head in a ponytail, exactly the way I had taught him. I found it hard to do his hair every day by making a bun on his head and then covering it with a *patka* (headcloth). Cutting the hair was not allowed.

MADAM MOHINI - A Romantic Tale of Violence

During the day, he sauntered around the house, picking at this, nibbling at that. I did not have to tolerate his wicked laugh and reckless clowning anymore. There were other servants to do that now. His violent behaviour towards me was all sorted out in the bedroom. After dinner, he would bolt out of one room and enter another. He would cling to his mother sometimes. His mother would shoo him away and tell him to go to his bedroom.

I would be standing in the doorway, waiting for him to un-grip his mother and come in with me.

'Go, my son, my little son,' she would say in a cajoling tone. I did my best not to look up, not to give her any clue as to what was going on. I kept my eyes down and said nothing to him. Last night when I was waiting for him in the same way, I tried to flash my eye at him. Pammi saw that. My heart jumped and my eyes fluttered. I quickly occupied myself with staring at the floor and looking suitably bashful.

I had settled things once and for all on the very night of our wedding. He was pushed inside the room by his mother. He wore a cream silk *Kurta pyjama*. I locked the door and kept the key under the mattress and let free a frightful blow on his mouth. The force of it almost knocked him off the floor. His body flung across the bed. For a moment, he lay stunned, dark blood oozing from his nose and saliva dripping from his mouth. A very faint whimpering sound came out of him. Then he rolled over and raised himself shakily on all fours.

MADAM MOHINI - A Romantic Tale of Violence

I picked up a baseball bat and raised it, 'Dare you shout and I will crush your skull to pieces,' I muttered in a low voice out of my clenched teeth. He sat very still. His knees close to his chest and hands crossed about his knees. His face became pale. I am sure he would have been wondering what he had done to deserve that. I couldn't believe that it was so simple to tame him. He had no choice but to take it. He dared not touch me ever and slept meekly on the floor while I slept on the soft mattress in bed like a queen. I made it very clear to him that the one with a louder voice did not always command.

Thereafter, I could always feel his stomach muscles clenching when I shot him a sharp glance. He was usually cheerful during the days, playing cricket and hooting playfully. He played music and danced merrily. It was easy to stop him from doing what I didn't want him to do. It generally took not more than a shake of my head or a cold hateful look in my eyes. He tried to linger around his mother as far as possible. He stuck to her more when he sensed that she was going out. 'Come on Jeetu, go and play,' she sounded irritated. He held her arm nagging. She slapped the back of his hand, 'I will be back soon. Now let go.' An impatient look flashed across her face. I was arranging roses in a flower vase on the coffee table on the veranda when this scene was going on. He shook his head. I could see from the corner of my eye that he was glancing at me again and again; his head tossing nervously. She turned to me.

✦ 219 ✦

'Mohini, he is behaving in a strange manner. Is everything fine?' she frowned and looked deep into my eyes. I cringed and immediately cast my eyes down. It was the safest bet. I couldn't trust my eyes to feign normalcy and I knew her cleverness all too well.

'Yes, all is fine.' I said smoothly without any hint of a stammer. I felt proud of myself for being able to lie so glibly.

'And how many times have I told you to call me mommy?' She said irritatedly.

'Right,' I looked up at her.

She shook her head and left. I could never call her mommy. The word just did not match her. I glanced around. Servants were working all around.

'Why do you do this Jeetu? Never do it again. Ok!' He smiled. The tension on his face eased. He swayed his upper body from side to side and giggled.

'That's a good boy.' I called a servant to play with him and he hopped away happily.

That night at dinner, Jeetu was sucking on a chicken bone. As usual, Gursimran had not yet come home. Pammi's fingers were working the meat off a bone. She was engrossed in her own mind. Jeetu made a gesture for another serving.

'You have eaten four bowls of chicken curry, Jeetu. You should stop now,' I said chewing on a morsel.

He produced an insisting squeal. His overeating was more of a problem to me than to him. He farted all night and made the air unbreathable. Many times, I would have to open the window to be able to breathe. With his belly overfed, he did another weird thing. He would snort like a horse while sleeping. Displaying the rows of yellow teeth inside, his mouth would open and close like a fish outside water.

'No, you have had enough,' I pressed. He gave an escalated squeal mixed with anger.

'What?' I looked at him questioningly.

He leapt at the empty bowl of chicken and hurled it at me. I was more astonished than furious thinking how did he dare. His mother pacified him, 'No, my son. This is not fair,' she gently wagged her curry-stained finger at him. He continued squealing and growling at me. I looked perfectly calm, and not at all perturbed.

I surveyed the curry stain on my shirt and started rubbing it off with a napkin. I forced a plastic smile on my face, meant for his mother in case she was looking at me. It was not meant for him. I did not even look at him. I analysed, that his behaviour was encouraged by the two polite sentences I had spoken to him in the morning. It set him believing that the old times were back, that he could do all that to me as he did earlier. Though I was fully consumed by anger at that time I maintained the smile on my face. *Good*, I praised myself as I walked out of the dining room.

That night, as soon as he entered the bedroom, I gave him a murderous stare. I snarled while advancing towards

MADAM MOHINI - A Romantic Tale of Violence

him. Instinctively, his arms crossed over his face, where I had struck him the first time. I lunged at him, grabbed his arm, and dragged him down onto the floor. He opened his mouth to howl. I immediately gagged his mouth with one hand and gave the first blow in his belly. I slapped his face, wrung his ears, and pulled his hair. He was writhing his body this way and that. He was weeping and wailing silently. I gave a final kick on the bone at the base of his spine. 'Will you ever try to hit me?' I whispered strongly in his ear. He shook his head frantically. He was quivering uncontrollably. I hurled abuses at him in a low voice, all the popular ones relating to mothers and sisters. Since he had no sister, I limited the repertoire to the mother ones only. These are the most famous among Punjabis. They say them because it sounds cool and needs no imagination. I was amused at how easily I could utter them. I have grown up hearing these abuses but had never got a chance to let them ride on my voice.

Thereafter, he became remarkably docile. He had learnt the consequences of annoying me. He shivered with fright when I sneered or shot a glare of bloodshot eyes at him. He tried his best to avoid me during the daytime. He turned back whenever he saw me in the corridor or on the stairs. When we crossed in a doorway and our bodies happened to brush each other, a surge of terror filled him and he hurried away from me.

When his mother was not at home, he would sit somewhere, where the chances of my going were limited.

✦ 222 ✦

MADAM MOHINI - A Romantic Tale of Violence

He would sit there sulking and feeling desolate. I was enjoying it. The cruelty made me cheerful. Initially, I had felt scared of my own cruelty. But the truth is that I didn't altogether hate it. I liked how it felt to curse him, beat him, to have a target at which I could focus all my simmering frustration and grief.

* * * * * * *

It was a wet winter morning. Jeetu and Pammi had gone somewhere. The year was ending. It was raining. I sat on the veranda watching the windswept bottle palms of the garden. A gust of wind hurled the dead leaves from the curved hedge. A pair of sparrows sat close to each other under a thick bunch of leaves on the mango tree. They were wet and shivering. Bahadur came with two cups of tea and *pakoras*.

Whenever there was no one at home, we often sat together and talked. I took the cup in my hand and felt its soothing warmth. The wind sprayed us with rain. The chill caused a tickling sensation on my skin. I pulled my shawl up around my neck to protect against the chill. The amazing softness of the shawl warmed me fast. 'It is an expensive one' Pammi had told me while giving it to me, 'it is made of Shahtoosh wool'.

'I have never seen you wearing that green sweater which I had brought for you,' I asked Bahadur.

'It makes me sweat,' Bahadur said while looking at the glistening drops of falling rain.

✦ 223 ✦

MADAM MOHINI - A Romantic Tale of Violence

'Even in this chill!' I exclaimed.

'Yes.' He nodded his head.

'This is the magic of money,' I said and both of us smiled feebly at each other.

'Make yourself busy in better things other than ambling about in the house,' he said to me.

I wiped the droplets of mist from my eyelashes, deposited by the last spray. Bahadur was pushing a *pakora* round and round on the plate. My eyelashes fluttered.

'Hmm...I need to,' I replied plainly, though my voice was mysteriously resolute.

It was evening. Jeetu and Pammi had still not returned. It rarely happened that she took Jeetu along and even rarer that they stayed out for so long. I was sensing some change in the atmosphere over the last few months. Sometimes Pammi stared at me and sometimes she frowned at me. Sometimes she gave me a sharp searching look. I leaned out of the window, resting my elbows on the sill to see if their car was back. I could see cars parked beyond the low boundary wall on the wet black street. But the driveway was bare. It was still raining. I heard the tip-tap of drops on the green fiberglass awning of my window.

'What could it be?' I thought hard and my mind went back to a conversation I had overheard one day. She was on the phone.

'He is scared all the time,' she was saying. There seemed to be a doctor on the other end. '...and always

✦ 224 ✦

MADAM MOHINI - A Romantic Tale of Violence

looks frazzled. He has stopped playing music as well and he always seems panic-stricken.'

The wind picked up and hissed past the window. I felt the tip of my nose freezing.

Lying in bed, I pulled the quilt up to my neck. *Perhaps, her diabetes is keeping her queasy*, I thought. Since the time she was diagnosed with diabetes, she was rarely in a good mood. I lay limp in the bed staring at nothing. This was becoming boring. I had nothing to do. I was no more than a creaking door hinge, a patter of sandals on the floor, or a splash of water in the washroom. Occasionally, she would take me to the market in a chauffeur-driven Fiat Contessa car and I shopped and shopped for silks, pearls, fancy sandals, fashionable purses, expensive perfumes, and branded cosmetics. I shopped till my head throbbed with boredom. I had everything. I had more than any woman could have. I wondered how Pammi had such an incredible appetite to shop. She had started so many years back and was still doing it.

Pammi's authority was absolute in the house. She did not act upon her instincts but knew clearly what was needed to safeguard her position. I had no discretion in the house save which colour bed sheet or curtains I wanted in my bedroom or choosing the channel on my bedroom TV or choosing the flowers in the vase in my bedroom. For the rest of the house, it was her choice. She wanted roses on the veranda, lilies in her office,

✦ 225 ✦

MADAM MOHINI - A Romantic Tale of Violence

and carnations in the dining room and that is what was done. The food was cooked to her taste more so since she became diabetic. Like a driver takes time to adjust to the light outside after driving through a long dark tunnel, the same way it took me some time to adjust to the riches. And soon it all started feeling normal, it was nothing out of the world. The only exception was the few visits to my house in the village in a car with a driver. I never ventured out of the house alone; I was not allowed to. Her instructions about this came a week after the wedding.

'I will gladly accompany you to any place you want to visit. Going out alone, for a bride of such an honourable family, is not graceful.' The sternness of her words was masked by politeness. The change in her behaviour was initially bewildering but it also made me believe in my elevated status. The only place she allowed me to go alone was to my village. Apparently, she was not willing to be seen in a village in front of a shabby abandoned house. She pretended to be extremely busy whenever I asked her about the visit.

Visiting my house had increasingly become an exercise in agonising myself. It was like re-living the whole trauma of that night. I scrambled frantically to commit it all to my memory of what happened that night. I felt rattled at how time was trying to blur the details of my memory. What did those policemen scream? Did they tell her that they would take her into custody?

MADAM MOHINI - A Romantic Tale of Violence

Her screams pierced my ears and the tremendous pang of that original pain returned. Were they raping her? And a maddening rage surged in me. I would kick the wall or bang my fists on the floor. Then those moments would pass leaving me deflated, dissipated.

Squatting on the bedroom floor, I would look up at that squarish opening in the ceiling the shutter of which had gone now, sunlight beaming in brazenly forming a bigger square of light on the floor. Then a pang of strange and indescribable guilt interlaced with the pain. I should not have gone to the roof. I should have stayed with her. Whatever had happened to her would have happened to me as well. At least, I would have saved myself from this killing tormenting wait for her.

Then I made ground plans. *In case she is in prison, they might have put her under a trial before passing a sentence*, I thought. I would talk to the Prime Minister or the President or the Chief Minister. I would write letters to them seeking their help. Then I imagined myself going to them, each one of them and pictured myself being pushed away from the gates. I saw myself on the verge of tears, my head drooping like the ears of an Afghan hound and then I saw myself retracing my steps.

I dropped the idea of sending letters as it was easy to imagine what would happen to them if at all I wrote. They would end up in the garbage. My thoughts never stopped meandering around these plans as long as I was

✦ 227 ✦

MADAM MOHINI - A Romantic Tale of Violence

at my house. It always took me some days or sometimes even weeks for that sorrow to diffuse.

I got the hole in the back wall plugged and the window panes fixed. I got the house cleaned and the walls whitewashed. Then I found myself thinking, 'Now what?' I felt weak and powerless. The feeling of debility would trigger a series of newer horrifying ideas. It took me a great effort to shut my mind off them. So, I decided to stop these excruciating visits, at least for now.

The chilled wind was shooting in from the window and my body shivered even in the quilt. I came out of bed to shut the window. A glance at the driveway and I saw her car there and Gursimran's behind it. After a few minutes, I heard her shouting. Gursimran's voice was tentative and muffled. Then I heard a door open violently and close with a bang. Heavy footsteps were pounding on the stairs. And then my door burst open and Pammi came through.

She shot a sharp look at me which hit me like a piece of broken glass.

'I knew it. It's you,' she snarled and advanced towards me.

'What are you talking about,' I stammered and began backpedalling.

'I should have known,' she spat out. 'You worm of a gutter! A dog can't stop eating filth even if it sits on a throne. I should have known this'. She grabbed my arm and gave a hard slap on my face. It felt like a

MADAM MOHINI - A Romantic Tale of Violence

solid iron plate. My brain shook violently and my head started spinning. The room was reeling up and down. Everything became hazy. Her face looked double its size and her bloodshot eyes seemed ready to swallow me. I could see her lips moving but couldn't hear anything. After a moment it was just sound, 'I should have known this. You are ruining my son'. She raised her hand again.

'No...No...don't do this,' I pleaded but she hit me again, this time on the other cheek. It shook me off my feet and sent me flat on the floor. I was too stunned to do anything. She pulled me by my plait and I stood up shakily.

'The Doctor says, my son is still a virgin, you bitch!' She screamed at me.

I shivered with fright when she sneered and tightened her fist and the next moment it was in my belly. I doubled up with pain and rolled on the floor. That unbearable pain anaesthetised me. After that, I didn't feel the pain of all the kicks and slaps she delivered on me. She continued thrashing me till she herself was huffing. A last murderous stare and she left the room.

I stayed on the floor for a long time. I was feeling too dizzy to stand. When the faintness started giving way to sense, the ache in my jaw was unbearable. My mouth was sticky and tasted evil. I finally stood up and looked in the mirror. My teeth were bloodstained like those of a knocked-out boxer. One side of my cheek flesh was darkening. My face had swollen and looked like a

✦ 229 ✦

MADAM MOHINI - A Romantic Tale of Violence

shapeless ball of wheat dough. It ached everywhere — my neck, face, shoulders, and belly. My mind was dazed, incapable of thinking coherently. Then slowly I pulled myself together and calmed myself.

I sat limply on the edge of my bed. The light outside faded and the trees deepened. I was no longer frightened or agitated, just thoughtful, thinking deeper and deeper. I quietly stepped out of my bedroom and slowly walked to the back lawn and out through the back gate. The sky was still overcast and the breeze was bone-chilling. I hugged myself against the cold and walked slowly on the rain-soaked walkway, my mind deeply engrossed in thought. The physical pain was under control; instead, a feeling of humiliation gripped me.

I slowly lowered myself onto the ground with my back against a tree along the sidewalk. The city was amazingly silent save the sounds of trucks swishing by on a distant watery road. Windows were glowing dimly. Street lights were off as usual. Here and there a dog barked reluctantly. A shudder passed through me. A current of something sad and forlorn. Suddenly, I missed my mom with such an overpowering intensity as I had not missed her since those terrible days in Delhi. It was followed by a recklessly wild thought. *She can't get rid of me even if she so thinks,* I thought to myself.

The next morning, I made myself stand before Pammi with folded hands and neck hung to my chest and made myself say, 'I am sorry. I repent'.

MADAM MOHINI - A Romantic Tale of Violence

She looked at me sternly, 'I want a grandson,' she ordered.

'Yes, but forgive me first.' With this, I flung myself at her feet looking absolutely devastated and repentant.

'That's all right,' she placed her hand on my shoulder and pushed it gently.

'I must serve you; you are my mother-in-law, my mother,' I pushed the last two words out of me before they could stick in my throat. Then I wondered what else to say. I looked up. Her face had a victorious delight.

* * * * * * *

Since I had got married, I had plenty of time on my hands. I spent that time idling around and watching TV programmes that showed lions hunting and hyenas robbing them of their hunt; dogs having sex, monkeys mocking, and shiny snakes slithering in the woods. I should have spent that time thinking and planning, all the thinking that I was doing now when I was totally screwed up and had very little time to do anything substantial. Without losing any time, I embarked on a new mission routine of flattering her from the morning tea to the time she went to sleep at night.

The next morning, I stood at her bedroom door, 'I made tea myself, ginger tea, Mommy ji. This is good in winters.' I stood with a kettle and two cups on the tray.

MADAM MOHINI - A Romantic Tale of Violence

'You need not do all this. What are the servants for?' Gursimran said while giving final touches to his turban. His wife just came out of the washroom.

'This gives me pleasure. I have not done it in a long time now, I guess,' I said.

'Let her if she wants to,' she cut down my speech and settled in the chair for tea. I turned to go.

'Come on, join us,' she said lazily.

I glanced at the two cups.

'I have had tea. You go ahead,' said Gursimran.

I sipped the tea in silence. I didn't want to say anything as it involved the risk of my fakeness getting detected. She was also quiet.

Later in the morning, just before breakfast was to be served, Shiela the maid, came to the kitchen. I was already there to see how I could show my care. Sheila opened the fridge door and took out a tiny bottle.

'What is this?' I asked looking sideways.

'Madam, this is Pammi Madam's medicine.'

'Oh! Insulin?' I asked her.

'Perhaps, Madam,' Shiela said, 'shall I go, Madam Ji?'

'Yes.' I replied.

Casting a quick look in the fridge I saw that there were some more of them. Later, I found out that she had to take a shot of insulin before every meal.

I kept flattering her over the next few weeks from telling her how fine her manners were to how fair her

MADAM MOHINI - A Romantic Tale of Violence

skin was to how it was obvious from her walk and gait that she was destined to enjoy riches. She bloated with pride and lapped up all the praises. I kept admitting my folly of being blind to such a blessing of having a mother-in-law like her. I normalised my relationship with Jeetu as well. I stopped giving him those stares and hard looks. He was less scared of me now. His behaviour kept sending muted signals of normalcy to Pammi. One night after dinner, I was massaging her feet. Earlier, this had been Shiela's job but I took over from her because it looked like an exercise that symbolised complete surrender. This was sure to make her believe that I was on her desired track.

'So, when am I going to hear the good news?' she suddenly asked while reading the *Political Weekly* magazine. Of late, she had started reading magazines with heavy-sounding names which made others feel that she had her fingers on the pulse of the nation and that her being was crucial for the nation's well-being.

'What are you talking about, Mommy Ji?' I said perfectly politely with absolute innocence.

'You know what I mean,' and this time she looked at me. 'When did you have your last periods?' she asked.

I fixed my gaze at her feet yet I could see from the corner of my eye that she was still looking at me. I could not evade the question for long.

'They are going on right now,' I said and massaged more dutifully. I cleared my throat and said, 'Next

◆ 233 ◆

month... if God so wills.' I hated the stammer in my voice when I said that. I had thought of most things and had ready answers but this one genuinely baffled me.

That conversation set me thinking. How could I get pregnant? I hated Jeetu. He smelt of onions. His sweat had a smell of homemade yogurt gone bad. As soon as he entered the bedroom, the air would turn stuffy. It became worse when he farted. I could never bring myself to even touch him. The thought of having sex with him made me retch; I felt disgusted.

Though in some corner of my mind I envied his innocence. He knew nothing of what his mother wanted him to do. His naivety insulated him from the worries of the mentally able. He was like a lotus, staying aloof in the muck. Even at that age, his concerns were just eating, sleeping, and making merry like a child unless I gave him a spiteful sneer.

It was now clear that warming up to Pammi should not be the only task my mind should be working on. I had to put my mind into a rigorous exercise mode.

Next morning...

'Mommy Ji, I want to buy some books to read.' I told her innocently.

'Sure, we will go to the market some time.' She replied.

Our car pushed through the crowd. The driver was honking ceaselessly. We were in the small standard Maruti 800 car because the market was on a very narrow street

MADAM MOHINI - A Romantic Tale of Violence

and could be reached only after crossing many more such streets jammed with people, cycles, rickshaws, and scooters. The streets were made narrower by the carts of fruit and vegetable vendors who parked their mobile shops anywhere. A man driving a bullock cart was in front of us. It was loaded with a pile of rotting and leaking tomatoes, a swarm of flies humming over it. The cart made a rattling noise with its wooden wheels.

'Oh! Shit. Roll up the windows,' said Pammi frowning.

I cringed.

The cart crawled on. The man turned to the side every now and then and spat. *Was it a bad idea to come here for books?* I thought. *Am I not annoying her unnecessarily?* To my relief, the cart turned into one of the numerous streets which branched off the main street. The old part of this city is a baffling network of streets — narrow, narrower, and the narrowest. This is a beautifully unplanned city. More beautiful is the freedom that its people enjoy. The freedom to break rules on the streets and roads and the freedom to use any common public place in the ugliest possible way and dump garbage wherever they find a place.

I watched a stray cow ruminating, sitting near a pile of garbage. White foamy saliva was dripping from the sides of her mouth. Its tail was swatting flies away from its butt. I watched a barber shaving a man's beard, a small boy selling cheap rice crackers, smoke rising

MADAM MOHINI - A Romantic Tale of Violence

from the cigarettes. The car stopped. Keys clanged in the key chain. 'Go and quickly buy the stuff,' Pammi said sounding restless. I glanced at her and nodded. She slouched in the car seat.

Tens and thousands of books were there, books on all significant sounding *'logies'*. A smell of paper and glue. I asked for books on health and moved in the direction the shopkeeper pointed. I went through the titles as fast as I could. Some of the titles were not making any sense. A frantic search and my eyes landed on the topic I was searching for *Madhumay Atey Ilaz* (Diabetes and Its Cure). The book was in Punjabi and that was what I wanted. I picked it up and started searching again. I don't know why but I was getting panicky? Thankfully, I spotted the other one soon, *For The Mothers-to-Be*. It was in English but it didn't matter. It was not to be read anyway. I paid the bill and rushed back to the car. She glanced at the books and smiled at me. She seemed truly impressed. I felt like giving myself a good round of applause.

At night, I dug my eyes into the book on diabetes. An hour passed. Nothing meaningful was hitting me. I rubbed my eyes. They were burning from squinting at the book. I went to the washroom, splashed my eyes with fresh water, and started again. Jeetu was grunting in his sleep. His relaxed body on the carpet was in such a level of tranquillity, which was never possible for me to achieve. My mind went back to the book. I flipped

MADAM MOHINI - A Romantic Tale of Violence

the pages impatiently...flip...flip...flip. At last, I stopped at a page. My eyes widened. A shrill but subdued sound came out. I started reading it. My face scrunched up with concentration. It was about the cautions to be taken while using insulin. I read it over and over. A smile lingered on my lips till I finished reading.

All was set in my mind. I had to just wait for Gursimran to go for a night out and that day came sooner than I had imagined.

I followed Sheila to the kitchen after dinner for I knew what she was going there for.

'Shiela, I will warm up the milk for Mommy ji,' I said politely.

'Yes, Madam.' She nodded.

She busied herself in cleaning the kitchen. Bahadur was eating dinner squatting on the floor. I began heating milk in a pan, readied two cups, added a spoon of sugar in one, and then stole a split-second glance at both of them. Bahadur was looking at his plate and Shiela had her back towards me. I added four sleeping pills to the other cup, added milk, and stirred. 'Shiela, this red cup is for Mommy ji, without sugar,' I told her while handing over the tray. She took them. I followed her. My heart was thumping. Pammi took the red cup and drank the milk without a frown. The other cup was for Jeetu. He finished it too.

'Jeetu ji, you go to our room. I will be there shortly,' I told him.

✦ 237 ✦

MADAM MOHINI - A Romantic Tale of Violence

Then that usual foot massage routine followed. 'Mommy ji, I have read that foot massage is good for diabetics.'

'Yes, I know,' her voice was blurring.

'Mommy ji, I think you are sleepy. Stop reading this and go off to sleep.' I told her innocently.

'You are right.' And the next moment she was snoring. I stayed in her room, waiting for everyone to retire for the night. There was still some activity going on in the kitchen. Then I heard the kitchen door closing and the servants going to their quarters. My mouth was dry. My legs started trembling. I inhaled deeply and exhaled slowly to calm myself. I took out two bottles of insulin from my bra. I stood up on my shaking legs and steadied myself.

Calm down... Calm... I instructed myself. I picked up the insulin pen lying on the side table and filled it up with the medicine from the bottles. I tiptoed towards the door and stood there for two minutes. There was no sound outside. All was quiet. I bolted the door and came back to her. My hands were sweating. I took a deep breath again, rubbed my hands on my shirt, and tightened my grip on the pen. I willed myself to focus, focus on the bulge of her arm just below her shoulder, and then emptied the contents of the pen into her fat arm. The veins at my temples were threatening to burst. My whole body was trembling. I walked to the door soundlessly, gave her a last look, and left.

MADAM MOHINI - A Romantic Tale of Violence

Jeetu had slept. Lying in my bed, I kept staring at the ceiling fan. Her face, as I had seen it last, came back to my mind. She was so powerless. My heart was melting and whatever anger I had felt for her was passing. A mix of terror and guilt came over me. Then I saw the ceiling fan coming down closer and closer to my face. I was panting. The air was being sucked out of the room. And then it receded, receded farther and farther into the sky, into the stars. I couldn't move.

My limbs felt heavy as though made of stone. I was trying to breathe. The walls were breaking away. I was trying to scream but it stuck in my throat. Then someone shook me violently and my eyes opened with a jerk. I sat up. My body was sweating. I flung the quilt away and rushed to open the window and started inhaling frantically as though the world would soon run out of air. Then it slowed down. Slowly, it was all sound and colour. The sun was coming up and the birds were chirping. Jeetu was sleeping. I rolled back into bed and decided to wait.

An hour later, I heard wild thumping of fists on my door. Sheila was there, her eyes wide and shocked.

In Pammi's bedroom, a whole army of servants was standing, shocked.

'Call the doctor,' I shouted, 'Call Papa ji,' I added
After half an hour.....

'She is no more,' the doctor's eyes fluttered. 'Sugar went fatally low,' he told a shattered Gursimran.

MADAM MOHINI - A Romantic Tale of Violence

Jeetu sat near his mother's body, his hands in his lap, calm and motionless. His face was thin and drawn. A sudden feeling of remorse welled up in me. For days after that there was a constant tug of war in me regarding my feelings — remorse and guilt on one side and victory on the other. In the end, 'victory' won. This was how I learnt the foremost doctrine of politics — finish the invincible opponent. And soon, I was enjoying all her powers. Later, I would learn that power is addictive and once you have enjoyed it, its absence keeps you perpetually restless.'

Sukhbir's mouth was gaping. His gaze was fixed on Madam's unwavering concentration. He could see the reasons behind her hard-shelled composures since he had known her. He did not utter a word, but the eagerness of his eyes wanted her to continue speaking.

* * * * * * *

Chapter 10

'I heard Jeetu groaning feebly in his sleep. I woke up and took his head on my lap. 'Don't cry Jeetu, I am here.' He winced and his whimpering became louder. I patted his head patiently like a parent does to his child. After a few moments, he calmed down. Thankfully, this exercise became less time-consuming than before. It had started soon after his mother's death. He would start screaming in his sleep. It would take me hours to pacify him. At times, he would turn violent. His body would shake. He would bang his head on the wall. I had to call for help to control him. Gradually, his fits of terror and rage became weaker. Partly because more than a year had elapsed since his mother's death and partly because I set him thinking in a new direction.

The day his mother died he sat still by her side. I went near him. I heard him groaning faintly. Then suddenly, his hand was groping for some arm to hold, something to lean on. I presented myself. A choking voice came from his throat and the next moment he was weeping

✦ 241 ✦

MADAM MOHINI - A Romantic Tale of Violence

aloud. Oh! That was really unnerving. To my own surprise, I felt sorry for him and it set me weeping too.

I was glad that I did cry because I was expected to shed those tears. The consequences of this action were not bad either. One, I earned people's sympathy, and two, it made Jeetu believe that we shared a common sorrow. I caressed him and stroked his head gently many times a day for days after her death. He often winced and complained of an aching head or stomach or ears. The doctor was sent for, medicines were given. He looked relieved for a day or two but then the pain would revive. No one knew whether the pain was real or imaginary, yet everyone including me dutifully cared and tended to him. The possibility of real pain was never denied. After all, he was the son of a Minister.

He lay in bed for days together, picking at his hair or scratching his beard. I tried to entertain him with various activities like dribbling a basketball or making clownish gestures. I coaxed him out of bed but I found him staggering through the house. He always ended up in his mother's room which ran the risk of him becoming out of control with anger. Many times, I had rescued him from that room. He would wrap his arms around me and cry. I looked at his face. I was startled to see his cheeks looking sallow and his eyes, deeper. There was a gaping space between his neck and the collar.

He started hovering around me the whole day. He held me by my elbow or gripped the edge of my

MADAM MOHINI - A Romantic Tale of Violence

dupatta and refused to go away. Perhaps, he felt a sense of security from me. Perhaps, he was trying to fill the vacuum created by his mother's absence with me. It was exhausting to endure him throughout the day but I didn't lose patience because a plan had cropped up in my fertile mind and it required me to remain calm.

I spent days looking after him. I dragged my feet around the house, down the corridor, on the lawn, or wherever he wanted me to take him till he himself got exhausted.

It was a cold winter morning. The sun lingered in its sleep and even after waking up, chose to lie under the blanket of soft grey clouds. Jeetu and I went to our room after breakfast. I began to tickle him in his armpits and he started laughing convulsively. He tried to kick me but I jumped off. He was so weak with laughter that he didn't even have the strength to push me away. I continued tickling him. His laughter became soundless and his cheeks turned red and hot. He made pleading gestures with his hands begging me to stop.

I stopped to let him catch his breath. Then I started again at his feet. He pulled his feet up with a jerk and rolled himself into a ball and started rolling on the bed. As soon as his breath normalised, he jumped off the bed and leapt towards me. I ran out of the room, down the stairs, into the lawn shouting, 'Sorry, sorry Jeetu Ji...' Jeetu was charged with excitement. He continued laughing. He laughed so much that his nose started running. He lifted an edge of his kurta and wiped it.

✦ 243 ✦

MADAM MOHINI - A Romantic Tale of Violence

I gestured a 'no.'

The frown on my face expressed my displeasure at what he had just done. His face fell. He gestured a 'sorry' by touching his earlobes and took a handkerchief out of his pocket and wiped his nose with it. Then he started dancing around in the garden, a kind of tap dance. At that moment, Gursimran's car entered the house and it had no beacon on it. He would remove the beacon and set the driver free, every time he went away at night to return in the morning. It was almost 10:00 am. He glanced at us. I wrapped my woollen shawl around my shoulders and pulled the dupatta over my head.

Jeetu ran towards him, uttering gleeful sounds induced by the recent bout of laughter. But Gursimran treated him with a strange indifference. As Jeetu advanced towards him in large strides, he turned and went off from the driveway and moved towards the drawing-room. Jeetu stood there in disappointment. A resentful frown appeared on his forehead and he started thumping his feet on the floor in protest. I quickly intervened and distracted him from his anger.

Now, Jeetu wanted to be around me all the time and I allowed him to do so.

That evening was as dull and cold as the day had been, but it was not biting cold. Low clouds hung over the city. A steady breeze blew from the east. The breath would turn into mist as it came out of our mouths. The air was weighed down by the clouds and I could feel

MADAM MOHINI - A Romantic Tale of Violence

its weight all around. As the sunlight faded, the breeze also stopped and haze started descending in the garden. I went into the kitchen. Bahadur was chopping *saag*.

'Isn't it late for *saag*, Uncle?' I asked while taking out a carrot from the vegetable basket. I washed the carrot and started munching on it.

'No, it is for tomorrow,' he replied without looking at me.

'Oh, what is for dinner then?' I asked.

'Carrots and sweet peas,' he replied plainly. 'Saab ji has a guest tonight. So, he asked me to cook the chicken too.'

'Guest? Who?' I enquired curiously.

'I don't know." He replied disinterestedly.

'Where is the guest?' I questioned him.

'In his office, I guess.' Bahadur answered without much concern.

I thought for a while and tried to guess who the guest could be? But before I could reach any definitive answer, I was already on my way to the office. I peeped in through the window of the living room to check if everything was well with Jeetu. He was sitting the way I had taught him, intently watching an old Hindi movie that had numerous songs and in which a moustached hero was seen twisting around a big hipped hopping heroine. They invariably moved round and round the trees. Then two big flowers were shown tapping into each other as a symbolic representation of them kissing.

✦ 245 ✦

MADAM MOHINI - A Romantic Tale of Violence

A typical artless romance. Jeetu enjoyed all this stuff. He was completely absorbed in the TV.

I heard a peal of laughter coming from the office. It was unmistakably that of a woman. Gripped by curiosity and confusion, I peeped through the narrow opening in the carefully drawn curtains. Yes, it was a woman. I was shocked. Her dark hair was tied in a knot at her neck. She was wearing a dark lipstick that sat on her lips like clotted blood and made her lips appear round and pulpy. She wore a loose red *salwar kameez* with a *dupatta* that clung to her neck. Her big breasts popped out brazenly from below the *dupatta*. I couldn't see Gursimran's expression as his back was towards me. But the way he swayed his body and moved his hands, it was more than obvious why she was there.

I was stunned at this unexpected and unwelcome development. I turned my eyes away from that distressful and distasteful scene. My future seemed to crumble before my eyes. For a moment I was in a state of limbo, having no idea what to do. There was a whole new army of questions in my head. *What if he marries this woman? What if she produces a pup? What if she takes away all that I hoped would be mine?*

What if...

What if...

'The 'What ifs' started buzzing in my ears like a swarm of million bees. I took long deep breaths to pull myself together and switched my mind into the

MADAM MOHINI - A Romantic Tale of Violence

'emergent thinking' mode. I was not ready to end with the exclamation, 'Of course! Why didn't you think of it before? It was so obvious.' I looked cluelessly into space. Everything seemed to be coated with a thin layer of mist and their contours were becoming indistinct by the minute. The veins at my temples were throbbing and I could feel the heat radiating from my cheeks.

I went into the garden and was soon enveloped in the thick fog. I walked slowly and aimlessly around the garden on the stone-paved walkway. A fine layer of moisture was settled on it. This was one of the rare quiet nights which happened only a few times a year. It was the first thick fog of the season. Most of the unwanted unsavoury noises were muted under the weight of the fog. No leaf was stirring. I could hear very faint sounds of utensils from the kitchen. But they were too weak to annoy me or distract me.

I felt strangely secure as my thoughts couldn't escape through this envelope of fog. I could think without worrying how my thoughts would manifest into expressions. I clenched my fists and shook them in frustration. I kicked the innocent trees which lined the walkway. After giving sufficient vent to the negative energy generated by fear and apprehension, I felt better and more stable.

I walked out of the back gate. The streets were deserted. Most of the numerous stray dogs had coiled themselves on the heaps of building materials that dotted

MADAM MOHINI - A Romantic Tale of Violence

the entire neighbourhood. Some of the more desperate ones let out a random bark. By being in the company of human beings for a long time, they had acquired two characteristics. One is the habit of barking even when absolutely unnecessary and two, is an urge for an all-season mating. Even a cold and quiet night like this could not quell their hunt for a mate.

I felt cordoned off from the world. No one could see me and I could see no one, nothing, except the street under my feet up to a few steps ahead. Street lights looked like just hazy spots of light hanging in space. This was heavenly designed privacy. Little droplets of dew settled on my hair. I touched them and felt the moisture seeping through my fingers and reaching every pore of my skin. It was amazingly tranquillising. My nerves instantly calmed down. I could think clearly and formulated two plans. One was the main plan and the second was a contingency plan which had to be set rolling in case the main plan failed.

I went back home. Everything was as calm and quiet as I had left it.

I couldn't sleep much that night and got up earlier than usual. It was 5:45 am. I went out and sat on the balcony of my room. I looked around. I could see nothing — no concrete, no electricity poles, no cables — nothing. There was just a white curtain of fog. Birds and dogs were still sleeping. A drop of water fell every five seconds from the awning onto the railing of the

MADAM MOHINI - A Romantic Tale of Violence

balcony. I sat there in absolute silence till I heard the sound of utensils in the kitchen. I got up and came back inside feeling armed.

I made it a point to be at the breakfast table before Gursimran. We normally never ate together. He always ate and left early while I was still warming up for the day.

'Ah! How come you are so early today?' Gursimran asked as soon as he saw me in the room. He was setting the collar of his white shirt under his black coat.

'Papa ji, I felt hungry,' I replied promptly. He settled down to eat. Sheila brought a *parantha* and Gursimran started eating. I cleared my throat. 'Papa ji,' I uttered faintly.

'Yes,' Gursimran's mouth was full.

I hesitated for a second and then said, 'I want to say something if you allow...'

'Sure, go ahead,' he said hastily.

'Though the matter is personal to you, since it is my duty, more so after Mommy ji, that I watch the welfare of this family,' I said in a profoundly concerned tone.

His chewing slowed down, though he didn't look up from his plate. An apprehensive frown flashed across his face. He didn't say anything. I took his silence as permission to go on and so continued speaking.

'Papa ji, I really liked that Aunty Ji, who was at our house yesterday. She seemed to be a nice and kind woman. But my small brain has come up with a

✦ 249 ✦

MADAM MOHINI - A Romantic Tale of Violence

suggestion which I would like to put forth.' I laid down everything very methodically. My gaze was fixed on his face to catch its every colour. He nodded a 'yes' though the morsel in his hand trembled. All going well till now. I took a deep breath and threw the final dice, 'Papa ji, this is an election year and your opponents are sniffing like wild hounds for issues. If only you would postpone any decision in this matter till the elections, you would be invincible.'

Something seemed to have shifted inside him. A shadow passed across his face. He stopped eating, got up and walked out of the room. I watched his receding back. He hadn't looked me in the eye. I seemed to have hit the nail on the head. I patted myself at the amazing calmness with which I had said all that. The flair was so genuine and natural. I was pleased with myself and an involuntary smile erupted on my lips.

But his silence was mysterious. I had executed the main plan. Had he expressed his agreement, I would have been spared from straining my mind over the contingency plan. I sat there motionless and quiet, but my brain was galloping like a horse with blinkers. I tied the reins of the horse to a pillar and stroked his neck. He tossed his mane. I murmured softly into his ear, *You have victory in your mane. Just have a little patience in your hoofs, sweetheart.* I rubbed my forehead and looked around the room. Everything was quiet. I watched out through the door. Rows of neatly pruned

MADAM MOHINI - A Romantic Tale of Violence

rose flower bushes gleamed dimly through the haze. And through that haze, Gursimran reappeared.

He stood in the doorway and said, 'You are right, beti. I am happy at your concern'. His voice was flat and then he just walked away. I sat dead still in the chair. The breath knocked out of me. My hands were clamouring to clap but I curled my fists inwards, my nails dug into my palms. I continued to stare at the door with wild eyes till long after Gursimran was gone. Never before had success greeted me so easily. I felt like dancing but I controlled myself with a conscious effort. I had bought sufficient time that too at throwaway prices. I felt a power in me; the power gained by tearing a human mind to pieces and then putting it together again in a new shape of your choice.

* * * * * * *

I lay low for the better part of the day. Those few minutes with Gursimran had drained a good amount of my energy. Hatred is definitely more exhausting than love. Jeetu hung around me lazily. He sat in the easy chair which was near the window in my room. The chair was upholstered with beautiful green leather. He was staring around aimlessly while scratching his head.

'What are you thinking, Jeetu?' I asked absent-mindedly. I had planned to say nothing. He sat back and started sobbing with his eyes fixed on the floor.

✦ 251 ✦

MADAM MOHINI - A Romantic Tale of Violence

'Oh!' I muttered, got out of bed, and sat beside him on the armrest of the chair. I brought his head close to my stomach and patted him.

'I know, you are missing Mommy ji,' I said and he started crying a little louder.

'I miss her too. Poor Mommy ji,' I paused to sigh, 'she died for want of love. Papa ji never took care of him.'

Jeetu winced as if a pain shot through his body.

'You are also diminished in his eyes. Nothing you say or do matters to Papa ji.' I said in a controlled voice. Jeetu was moaning softly under his breath as if trying hard to think. 'Nothing of Mommy ji remains in Papa ji's memory. How could he forget her so soon?' I grimaced as he looked up. I looked into his eyes and asked, 'Did you see her, Jeetu? The woman who came to our house yesterday.' I raised my eyebrows enquiringly. He nodded his mouth gaping open.

'Papa ji is going to marry her.' I made a clucking sound to express disgust. He squared his shoulders and lifted his head. Everything I said seemed to make sense to him. He looked at me, his big eyes questioning what can be done?

'How difficult is it to say 'hello' or 'bye' to your son as you return and leave home? Did you see how he ignored you yesterday?' I gave him a prolonged stare. I saw a flash of red in his eyes. I had managed to evoke the desired feeling in him just by one long glance and a

✦ 252 ✦

MADAM MOHINI - A Romantic Tale of Violence

few rightly chosen well-spoken words. I had won him over. He clung to me and whimpered. I stroked him gently in reassurance.

Gursimran was eternally busy. We hardly saw each other during the day. Sometimes we happened to share our meals with him in silence. He spent most of his day outside the home attending rallies, meetings, weddings, or funerals. Even when at home, he was never approachable. He was always immersed in a sea of human beings. If he did happen to cross his son somewhere in the house, he could hardly say a word or pass a smile as he was always deep in his thoughts. To Jeetu, he was like a poster with no caption. The vibes emanating from Jeetu conveyed to me that to him Gursimran's indifference was fast becoming intolerable, that he had an impulse to shout curses at the top of his voice. Hatred was slowly and steadily piling up in him.

There was a constant trickle of people coming to the house. Servants were busy because there was always something or the other to be done. Apart from regular meals, gallons of tea and tonnes of snacks were prepared and served to the visitors every day. Being so busy and in such a rush, they even ignored Jeetu sometimes. He would ask for something and it would take hours to be supplied. He would make a few jerky paces up and down the veranda and then sit back, disgruntled.

That night he sank on the edge of the bed, trembling with revulsion. I sat beside him and put my arm around

MADAM MOHINI - A Romantic Tale of Violence

his shoulders. I didn't utter a word. What was the need to speak when silence worked better? He lay in his bed that night, unable to sleep long after the lights were switched off. He shifted restlessly. I got up and switched the lights on.

'Come on,' I whispered, 'throw off your blanket. I will show you something.'

We put on our jackets and tip-toed out of the room. It was almost midnight. The house was dead silent, no clamour of voices, no click-clacking of slippers through the rooms, no crash of pots and pans in the kitchen. We went into the garden. Jeetu hugged himself against the chill. The night was clear and serene. The moon hung low and shone so brightly that even the colours in the garden were visible. Everything was tainted a mysterious blue. My eyes wandered along the hedge. The fragrance of the night queen sedated the air.

'There,' I said softly, pointing towards the huge bushes of bougainvillaea. He looked curious. I took him behind the bush where a cat had given birth to four kittens. A shriek of excitement was ready to escape him, when I uttered an emergent, 'Shhh.....' and he immediately muted himself. The shriek remained trapped in his throat. The kittens were small furry rolls of flesh with big sparkling eyes. They mewed so tenderly that it sounded like pleasant music.

'It just occurred to me that you might be interested,' I whispered. He nodded in excitement. We stayed there

✦ 254 ✦

MADAM MOHINI - A Romantic Tale of Violence

for some minutes. Jeetu touched and ran his hand over their soft fur, making indistinct sounds.

While walking back to the room, I said, 'Why don't you go and talk to Papa ji? Give expression to what you feel, what you need...' my voice was low but heavy with concern. I looked at his face. It appeared livid in the moonlight. He seemed to be consumed by some inner thoughts.

The next morning, I was in the kitchen, giving instructions to the retinue of servants when I heard a clamour from Gursimran's office. Then I heard Jeetu hollering and screaming. Gursimran shouted furiously. There were some more voices from people who tried to smother the eruption. I smiled inwardly. He could not be controlled by anyone other than me now. So, I delayed myself in the kitchen doing nothing. Bahadur gave me a questioning glance. I ignored it. When the hollering and growling did not stop in the next five minutes, I decided to intervene. When I reached the scene, Gursimran was livid with rage, his turban, dishevelled. He was wagging his finger at Jeetu furiously saying, 'I am your father. Is this the respect you have for me?'

Two of his men were trying to pacify him while Jeetu was crying out loud and hitting the wall violently with his fists. Another couple of men were trying to control Jeetu but in vain. I pulled a face-ripping with astonishment. As soon as Gursimran saw me, he shouted out instructions to me, 'Control him... Control him. Take him out of my sight.' I lunged at Jeetu and spread my arms around him.

'Jeetu, calm down...calm down...' he shook my hands off and continued screaming. I tried again, looking suitably adroit, 'No Jeetu...please calm down now.' And he mellowed down a bit and I took him to the next room. Bahadur was at the door. I told him to be with Jeetu till I returned. I went to Gursimran and asked him aside for a few minutes. He waved everyone out of the room. He looked completely distraught. I sat in front of him and before I could say something, sobs burst from his chest.

'I tried...' he whispered, 'why did you leave?' he was talking to his dead wife. 'He hit me today. Is this the day a father lives to see?' he fell quiet as his voice failed him. I had never seen him crying.

'Papa ji,' I tried to console him, 'don't worry. I will look after him. I will tell him to behave.' He was silent but the weight on his heart was clearly visible in his wet eyes. 'I understand, you are going through a tough time,' I whispered, my voice was as soft as snow. I left the room quietly, wondering how I had misjudged my free-spirited spouse. My heart was jumping with excitement. Jeetu was still filled with cold and hard fury. I held his hand and took him to our room. It was always safe to talk in there. He sat quietly but his eyes were dark with anger.

'Jeetu,' I said. He looked at me absently. 'You did well,' I jerked my shoulders, trying to puff up my chest.

MADAM MOHINI - A Romantic Tale of Violence

He was looking keenly at me but I kept silent. He put his hand on my shoulder and shook it which implied that he wanted me to speak. I took the cue and started, 'I would have done even worse, had I been in your place,' and I banged my fist on my thigh. 'Why does he have no love lost for you? You are his only son, damn it!' I spoke through gnawed teeth. My voice was icy. Jeetu whimpered in agreement.

'But you created a spectacle of the whole thing. You should have expressed your anger when Papa ji was alone,' I said in a very matter-of-fact tone. He looked confused. His brain was foggy. Many shades crossed his face, but the fury was the predominant one.

Jeetu looked very gloomy after that day. A pall seemed to be hanging over him all the time. He stopped hollering as he used to. One evening, Gursimran joined us at the dinner table. Resolution in his walk showed that he had made up his mind about something. He came to Jeetu and placed his hand on his head smiling pleasantly. I felt alarmed. Jeetu shook off his hand rudely.

Gursimran's smile evaporated, but he quickly regained his composure, 'My son, we will go for a long vacation after the elections,' he sighed. Jeetu stood up suddenly and strode out of the room without a glance. A glumness consumed Gursimran and he sank in the chair. He was crumbling. His eyes hollowed with gloom. His attempt, though a feeble one, to connect with his

✦ 257 ✦

MADAM MOHINI - A Romantic Tale of Violence

son had been brutally brushed aside. He looked at me in bewilderment. I nodded sympathetically but said nothing.

Having years of practice, I had become good at predicting Jeetu's moods, anticipating his reactions, and thus bracing myself up. While working on Jeetu, I learnt a lesson that was equivalent to a complete course in professional knowledge. It was that work on idiots for they constitute the masses and hence matter, offer them sops at whatever the cost, make promises with a tongue dipped in honey and they will put their energies at your disposal thereby, making you potent.

This acquired potency will give you the power to turn a petty scuffle into a street brawl or into a horrid holocaust, depending on your requirements. Our democracy has graduated from an overt autocratic democracy to a covert autocratic democracy. Earlier it took an enthusiastic vociferous repertoire of slogans to inflame passions. But now, a subtler 'tongue-in-cheek' kind of words, though unconventional, work better. Sometimes even silence works better than a spoken word.

It had been foggy for the last few days. The sun made some desperate though unsuccessful attempts to pop its head. The chill was biting. I had a bad cough which adamantly refused to go. That night I had just slipped into my quilt after taking steam to ease my choked lungs when I saw a flash outside. I wondered what that

MADAM MOHINI - A Romantic Tale of Violence

was. It became clear in the next few seconds that it was from the sky. The clouds gurgled aloud and the volume and depth of the sound indicated that they hung close to the roof. I glanced at Jeetu. He twisted and turned in his sleep. At times he let out a groan and muttered some words but they were empty and devoid of meaning. A rumble of thunder rolled again.

It immediately brought back memories of my childhood when winter rains spanned over weeks and sometimes even longer; when somewhere near the end of the year the sky descended lower and lower; all in shades of grey. Drops of rain trickled down incessantly. Streets were dotted with puddles of muddy water. Birds and stray dogs huddled in their hideouts.

My mom always welcomed this rain as it brought relief to me from cough and cold. I kept looking for excuses to stay home and not go to school so that I could stay in the quilt clinging to my mom or sit before the hearth as she cooked food. She would dash my tea with ginger and sweeten my milk with honey. She covered my head with a woollen cap and wrapped me up in layers of warm clothes. Mining the memory, I thought how long it had been since I had visited my house in the village. The house had too many memories, painful yet cherished.

I was brought out of my reverie by the spatter of rain on the roof, serving a musical treat to my ears. I took the quilt off my ears to let in the sound. The music

MADAM MOHINI - A Romantic Tale of Violence

caressed me to sleep. Whenever during the night, I turned and got into a semi-sleep state, I heard the music and rolled back to sleep feeling satisfied that the rain might continue till morning.

I lingered in the warmth of my bed till late morning. A steady cold wind was sweeping through the room. I noticed that the door of the room was half-open and Jeetu was not there. I again curled up under the quilt keeping only my nose out so as to breathe in the moist air. Suddenly, there was a violent knock at the door.

'Who is it?' I said irritably at that unwelcome disturbance.

'Come soon, *beti*.' It was Bahadur and there was a tearing urgency in his voice. I rolled the quilt down my face and asked lazily, 'What has happened now?'

'Come soon. There has been a fight again,' he paused for breath, 'between Jeetu and Saab ji.' He informed me and scuttled back down the stairs. I threw away the quilt, sulked at the ruined peace of the morning, put on my jacket, wrapped a muffler around my neck, and went down.

I reached Gursimran's room. What met my eyes was totally unexpected. I swear by God that I didn't plan that. For a moment I was too paralysed to even move. Gursimran lay motionless across his bed, bareheaded. Jeetu stood near him breathing heavily, shuffling unsteadily on his feet. He had strangled Gursimran with the saffron *siropa* which he wore on his head, so

MADAM MOHINI - A Romantic Tale of Violence

savagely that his eyes had nearly popped out of their sockets. I felt nauseous and dizzy. My brain became numb. My body froze. I was unable to lift my feet. They seemed to have turned into lead.

'Call the doctor...call the police...' someone shouted behind me. I stared at the spectre unable to believe what I was seeing. I was not sure if it actually had happened. Jeetu mumbled something, hanging his head. Then he cocked his head to one side and started sobbing. Tears rolled out of his eyes. My heart skipped a beat. He raised his hand towards me, a slight tremor in his fingers.

'Oh, what have I done?' I muttered silently to myself as Jeetu sank to the floor and started wailing. I swear again, it was not planned. It was destined. Even today, when I think of that morning, I break out in goosebumps. With his bare hands, he had killed a strong well-built man like his father. He had garrotted him to death with just a piece of cotton cloth.

After the commotion of the morning, the day unfolded into a deadly silence. Gursimran was taken for post mortem and Jeetu into police custody. I sat all alone on the balcony of my room feeling jobless. I sat back and looked aimlessly into space trying to figure out the repercussions of these latest developments. The street lay wet and bare. The raw soil was rain-soaked. The sky was rippled with shades of grey. The belly of clouds was still heavy. There was no bite in the cold anymore. The level of noise was low just like whispered

✦ 261 ✦

MADAM MOHINI - A Romantic Tale of Violence

conversation. A steady wind crawled and it felt good on my cheeks.

On the roof of the house across the street, a flock of mynas sat with their feathers fluffed up. The trees in the garden looked clean and bright. A gentle rain began to fall, raindrops creating ripples in the puddles of water on the street. I could see groups of people gathering and dispersing at the main gate after conversing with the gatekeeper and the policemen posted there. News reporters also turned up in search of some sensational information. The gatekeeper came with a message that the reporters insisted on talking to me but I refused to appear before anyone. They dispersed reluctantly, feeling vaguely cheated.

I was in a pensive mood all through the day. A monstrous feeling of guilt was attempting to consume me. That expression on Jeetu's face kept haunting me, how bereft he had suddenly appeared. A confused medley of images kept floating in front of my eyes. At last, I gave up fighting back the tears and they streamed out unchecked. I didn't even attempt to wipe them. Drawing the shawl tighter about my shoulders, I touched my fingers to my temples. A headache flicked cruelly, pressing like a needle through my scalp. Massaging my head, I turned to my bed and was instantly asleep.

I woke up in the hour between the night and the morning. I had a cramp in my stomach because I had not eaten anything the previous day. The city was

MADAM MOHINI - A Romantic Tale of Violence

shrouded in silence and wind lay coiled up in the trees. My head was clear at last, unclouded by grief. I could think logically and precisely. Gursimran was gone. He was gone and there was only one thing to do now. I lay unmoving in my bed, perfectly still and waited for a new day to dawn.

Gursimran was brought home from the hospital early in the morning. Party workers and Gursimran's aides were busy making preparations for the funeral. A thick pall of gloom had descended on the whole house. Soon the house was packed with people. Gursimran was kept in the veranda, washed and dressed. The people pushed and shoved as they made their way to pay their last respects. They pressed against each other. The compound was pulsating with people all donned in sparkling whites. I sat beside Gursimran, quiet and forlorn. Finally, the crowd moved in a huge procession to the cremation ground. Gursimran's head burst with a loud pop on the pyre. And a saga ended. But then a new one began when at the *Bhog* ceremony the Chief Minister declared me as Gursimran's political heir.

Gursimran seemed to have chosen a perfect time to die. Elections were a year away so by-elections for the seat vacated by him were announced. Riding on the wave of sympathy, I won comfortably. Again, all this was destined not planned.

A few months after the murder, I went to see Jeetu in the central prison. He was sitting still with his hands

✦ 263 ✦

MADAM MOHINI - A Romantic Tale of Violence

crossed about his knees. As soon as he saw me, he leapt towards me but was forcibly held back by the prison guards. It was a noisy evil-smelling place, filthy and crowded. Merely visiting such a place needed nerves. Jeetu sat silently against the wall. He kept on staring at me with his large mournful eyes. He tried to say something. His mouth opened and closed several times but he couldn't utter a word. His eyes looked absolutely lifeless.

I drew a deep breath, trying to keep myself composed and forced myself to look into his eyes. His grim face broke into tears and veins stood out on his forehead. I began to panic. Nervousness gripped my mind and a vague emotion was choking my throat. A dull pain rose in my belly. Unable to bear the flash of his eyes, I left the place in a hurry. I thought frantically about what to do. Pity was the ruling emotion at that time. I decided to bail out Jeetu by engaging a good lawyer to fight his case.

But as the days passed, my mind gradually cleared the superfluous emotions and the pain in my belly waned. I never went to visit him again.'

Sukhbir got up without a word, looked around then went out to fetch water. Both of them were silent. He looked at her. Her soft heavy hair was parted in the centre, brushed back from the narrow temples and had the darkness of glossy chestnut. Her skin displayed dull, wheatish sallowness ripened over the years. He

MADAM MOHINI - A Romantic Tale of Violence

always had this impression that her heart was entirely subordinate to her head. Her glance was artless but it also had a luxurious cunning. What made her heart rule her head now was not yet clear to Sukhbir? Dawn was about to break. Moonbeams were streaming in from the window. Sukhbir sank back into the chair. Madam looked attentively at him. Sukhbir sat still as a statue.

'You understand me?' she said.

'Never more, Madam,' he replied.

'But what happened now that you have decided to quit politics? I am troubled about it.' He looked at her questioningly.

'You have got it all out of me,' she sighed.

'I am glad you told me,' he said gently.

'Last month we went to Canada.' She informed him though he already knew.

'Yes,' Sukhbir gave an all-knowing nod because he was primarily involved in planning that visit.

The government of Punjab was about to launch a Micro Hydel Power Project scheme on its rivers on a POPO basis. The government would be buying 100% electricity that they produced at a mutually agreed price. It was to be a lucrative business, especially for NRIs as they are entitled to certain tax benefits. Since the inception of the scheme, letters and calls from NRI's were being received, requesting her to visit them and enjoy their hospitality. On the birth anniversary of Guru Nanak, the NRI's of Toronto invited her to be the

MADAM MOHINI - A Romantic Tale of Violence

chief guest to preside over the celebrations at Dixie. She saw the opportunity serving three purposes — business, holiday, and religion.

'Walking along the corridor that led to my office, I had passed two gunmen standing in the shadow of the wall. They saluted me. I was startled out of my thoughts. I peeped into my office. The Director and Principal Secretary of irrigation were already there and they were discussing something. As soon as they saw me, both of them stood up. I was not sure how much these people respected me, but they all saluted me. I was given to mistrusting everyone.

Momentarily, I caught the Director's eye. I somehow knew that he was thinking the same thing. An unmistakable message seemed to pass through our eyes. 'I know all' he seemed to be conveying. And then that flash of communication was gone. I was sure he couldn't be trusted. The Secretary was flitting through a file and made some quick markings on it with his pen.

As I declared the meeting open, the discussion started. The Director sat like a man poised between thought and action. He was a short turbaned Sikh. His fair pink cheeks shone out of his thickly bearded face. He started speaking first, 'I am so glad that we have received an overwhelming NRI response for the scheme.' He continued speaking with an obsequious grin on his face. He gave a fabulous statistical analysis of various proposals. He seemed to have laboured on them. Yet,

MADAM MOHINI - A Romantic Tale of Violence

his discourse was nothing but a heap of rubbish details. I could have questioned him all day without getting any real information.'

'Perhaps, I need to expatiate further,' he said curiously.

'I would prefer to speak to Secretary Sahib now,' I replied with stiff courtesy. He sat up straighter and opened his mouth to say something but I raised my hand to his face, indicating for him to remain silent. He fell quiet instantly and sat back in his chair.

I looked at the Secretary. He peered at me from the top of his spectacles.

'I have gone through the proposals, Madam, and have listed the ones which look profitable in my understanding. But there could be certain facts outside my vision which can best be deciphered by your good wisdom.' He spoke flatteringly.

And in his practical way, he handed over the file to me.

'Madam, just have a look at this,' he said with a quaint smile which was weighed down by his twirled moustache like the air is weighed down by overhanging clouds on a rainy day. His eyes gleamed behind his spectacles. I nodded in agreement and stood up. I shut my eyes in deep deliberation. My mind was blank, trying to make sense of what these two officers had explained. Their words had barely registered. I concluded there was no use in straining my mind over the babble they had just poured out.

✦ 267 ✦

MADAM MOHINI - A Romantic Tale of Violence

'You should accompany me to Canada,' I said pointing my finger at the Secretary. He nodded stoutly. An overzealous officer like the Director would certainly not suit my purpose.

The next week, as you know, we took the flight from New Delhi which halted at Brussels and finally landed at Toronto. Though it was only quarter past five in the evening, it was already dark. An extraordinarily chilled wind greeted us as we came out of the Pearson Airport. My nose froze instantly. I hugged myself to control the shiver which ran through my body and pulled the hood of my jacket over my head. A Sikh gentleman was waiting for us. He quickly stepped forward with folded hands.

'Welcome... Welcome,' he said excitedly while opening the door of his black Mercedes Limousine for me. The Secretary settled in the front seat.

'It is bitterly cold indeed,' I said absently.

'Maybe it is a lot for you but it's quite normal for us here,' said the Sikh gentleman trying to look at me from over his shoulders. 'My name is Sahib Singh,' he added urgently, 'Sardar Aulakh Sahib has sent me to welcome you and accompany you to the hotel to ensure you are comfortably settled,' he talked without stopping. Sentences poured out from him in an unending stream. 'He was busy making arrangements for your stay. He has already made your schedule in consultation with your staff,' he said rather cheerily, looking from the rear-view mirror.

'Who is Mr Aulakh?' I enquired though I was not much interested.

MADAM MOHINI - A Romantic Tale of Violence

'He is my Dad,' he grinned childishly. He was an unnecessarily enthusiastic man. With every sentence he uttered, he jumped lightly in his seat making me nervous with his driving. I sat back wondering when on earth would this fellow stop talking. I leaned forward and touched him gently on his shoulder. 'Young man, drive more carefully,' I said softly. He fell quiet, but just for a moment, and then started speaking to the Secretary who sat beside him. It saved him the labour of turning his neck back to look at me.

I looked out of the window. Freshly fallen snow had sheathed the whole city white like a shroud. 'It looks gloomy,' I said thoughtfully.

'There are so many good things here, Madam,' the man turned to me at once, 'you should see the city,' he boasted. I laughed lightly. Egged by my interest, he began to spin larger yarns for me.

'You must see the city,' he said again, more emphatically this time.

'Hmm...' I said at last. 'I am sure it might be good but surely Patiala is better.' I said determinedly.

'What?' he said incredulously. 'Once you have seen Toronto, Patiala will seem nothing more than a sleepy squalid town.' He finally cut himself short and changed the topic. 'The sun sets early around this time of the year. It has left for India and will return tomorrow.' He laughed lightly at his own joke.

I was not amused.

MADAM MOHINI - A Romantic Tale of Violence

'Here we are,' he said triumphantly as our car halted in front of a hotel in Down Town. A group of Indians was waiting in the lounge with welcome bouquets. I shook hands with all of them.

'Madam, you should relax over the evening,' Mr Aulakh said after the welcome ceremony was over. 'In case you need any help kindly contact me,' he said while handing his visiting card to her.

'Thanks,' I said courteously.

'Madam, I shall join you tomorrow morning,' the Secretary said stepping forward, 'my brother stays in Scarborough. I want to visit him there,' he added pleasantly.

'Oh! Good, go ahead,' I said.

At last, I was in solitude, feeling relaxed in being alone.

As I entered my room, I stepped on a thick soft carpet which sent a calming wave to my body. It was a spacious room full of glamour and finesse. Table lamps on bedsides glowed dimly, spreading a gentle hue over the velvet curtains. I took a hot shower in the spotless white of the washroom and slipped into my nightgown.

I pulled the curtains open. Everything outside lay in a wonderwork of moonlight and shadow. It looked as if a thin sheet of frosted silver covered everything, sending every object into a meditative serenity. It was an incredible silence, which I had never experienced before. I wondered how I carried such an insatiable hunger for

MADAM MOHINI - A Romantic Tale of Violence

silence within me. How I had grown to depend entirely on myself for companionship! I thought of the comment that I had made about Patiala in the limo and I realised that I didn't mean what I had said. It was an outcome of the long-acquired habit of pretence.

I was startled by the ringing of the phone.

'Yes,' I responded.

A woman on the other side spoke in highly accented English, 'Madam, one Mr Singh wants to see you.'

'What for?' I asked stiffly, already irritated at this unwelcome intervention.

'He says he wants to pass on some very important information to you,' she answered.

'Ask him to fix an appointment with my PA,' I stuttered.

'Please hold on,' she said and returned after two minutes. 'Madam, he says it is a personal matter. He must get this directly to you.'

I was silent for a moment as it took me time to make out what she was saying. I had started understanding the English spoken in an Indian accent to some extent but her speech was truly baffling for me.

'Madam, what should I tell him?' she said slowly letting each word fill her mouth.

'Yes, yes' I stammered, 'I will be there in five minutes,' I said and put down the phone abruptly. I tried to banish from my mind the alluring landscape sprawling in the moonshine and focused my mind on the current situation. I made up my mind to quickly do

✦ 271 ✦

away with the visitor. My limbs came into action and salwar, kameez, jacket, and shoes quickly found their place on my body.

I reached the waiting room. An old turbaned man with a flowing snow-white beard and a long black coat waited for me. His cheeks were slightly sunken and his eyes seemed sincere. As soon as he saw me a gentle smile appeared on his face and his eyes brimmed. I felt it strange but didn't pay much thought to it because the solitude back in the room was tugging at my mind.

'Yes, Sardar ji, what brings you here?' I asked in icy matter-of-fact words.

He opened his mouth to say something. His tongue moved over some words but nothing came out.

'Yes,' I said sternly, raising my eyebrows.

'Beti Sahib,' he uttered, at last, words choking his throat. 'Don't you recognise me?' his voice cracked. A sort of numbness stole over me. As for that voice, I could have recognised it even from my grave.

'Yes, I do,' I whispered softly rooted to the spot. My mouth gaped. Whether in shock or astonishment, I can't tell.

'I thought...' my voice failed me.

His voice was intense as he completed my sentence, 'I was dead!' and on his face a look past description.

'No, I escaped that night,' he answered and took an unsteady step towards me and took me in his embrace. Kind warmth flowed from his body and entered mine. It

MADAM MOHINI - A Romantic Tale of Violence

was a feeling beyond any words. I felt as if I had longed for this warmth forever. I wanted to soak it all in. I burst into unaccounted for tears.

'I could trace you only a few years back.' He shook his head struggling to get the words out. Then he hobbled across the room and sat on a sofa. I sat in front. Tears were flowing out of his eyes like two little streams and getting lost in his beard. He wiped his eyes and stared blankly into space for some time. He had grown frail. He was painfully still now.

A surge of emotions had clouded my eyes as I looked at him. I could feel the reverberation of affection that flowed out of him. I had yearned for this for so long, my soul writhed for it. My cheeks were also damp with tears that unleashed themselves breaking all restraints. I never knew I would feel this way if I ever met Akashdeep. He was dead to my knowledge. Then a moment of silence came over me and I asked him the question which mattered the most to me.

'Where is mommy?'

Hope gleamed in my eyes, the hope which had been waiting in my chest like life waits in the womb of a seed. All those years flashed before me. The years, I had spent tendering this hope, crafting it into a motivation that shaped my life, like, a rude chisel shapes a piece of solitary rock. Akashdeep's eyes were clouded with pain.

'They...' his voice failed him in the face of the enormity of what he was about to say, 'cruel beasts...'

✦ 273 ✦

MADAM MOHINI - A Romantic Tale of Violence

he faltered again, the words choking his voice. Then mustering all the strength, he had, he spoke softly, 'Those beasts killed her. They shot her.'

My heart stopped as if a knife had been driven through it. My hands and feet turned as cold as ice. That cruel little sentence struck me like a thunderbolt. Everything around me shattered and tumbled and that hope was gone. The ground heaved beneath my feet. That one moment was swollen into a million folds of agony. The pain in my chest was so intense that for an instant I was certain that my heart would stop beating.

Shuddering, he rose to his feet, came next to me, and stroked my head with his wrinkled hand. He stared crestfallen at the tears running down my cheeks. My eyes had turned into swollen roaring rivers threatening to swallow everything in their engorged path. He stepped closer to me and I rested my head against him. Memories came back to me in flashes, in disjointed but vivid images. For a long time we stayed like that in silence. Neither of us spoke. Both were lost in thought.

'They picked her up to know my whereabouts. But how could she have told them when even she believed that I was dead.' His face contorted with grief. 'I am sorry, Beti Sahib, I couldn't save her,' his voice cracked again. A heartbeat later, a surge of rage flashed on his face, 'But I didn't let them live either. Time had come for them to face the consequences of their godless ways. I shot them in the police station itself, in Jagraon.' He

✦ 274 ✦

MADAM MOHINI - A Romantic Tale of Violence

paused for a moment. I remembered the incident as I was there in Jagraon that night at Gurpal's house.

'Then, I escaped the country,' he sighed mournfully. 'There was nothing left; everything was ruined.' His eyes welled up.

I shut my eyes, so much weight was on my chest that for an instant I was certain that it would fall apart. I was so very tired. I was shackled to loss and grief. The lips of that wound never met and never healed. The hurt accumulating over the years had hardened and thickened my heart. I hauled it along, carried it on my back like a sack of stones. Revisiting that painful memory day in and day out had drained me; hollowed me out.

I felt my mother, felt the comforting rise and fall of her chest beneath my cheek, my arms tight around her, holding her as close as I possibly could. A deep voice came into my ears, 'forgive me.' He stopped to gather himself. He tried to say something but there were no words, just sounds of grief. Then he walked away. His legs seemed to grow leaden with every step.

My head felt heavy, unbearably heavy. I shifted sides in the bed trying to make myself comfortable but it was in vain. I looked absently at the ceiling. Then I sat up and kept pacing in the room, back and forth. I slid open the window. A light breeze flitted through stirring the curtains. I shivered but the chill didn't bother me. The road and the vast lonely forest beyond it were steeped

MADAM MOHINI - A Romantic Tale of Violence

in mourning. Trees had lapsed into irrevocable silence. It seemed as if everything had turned to stone. Trees seemed to grimace at me in the moonlight. The road sprawled forward but nothing was visible. A stench cascaded out of every pore of my body. The clock was striking. It sounded very loud in the snowy silence.

I sat staring at the dark window, waiting for the shimmer of dawn. At last, I saw a pale light coming up in the sky. I wrapped myself in the warms and looked out of the window, hoping to see someone on the road. But no one was in sight. The snow seemed to have conquered everything. It started snowing again, muffling the world in layers of thick white velvet. The silence was getting heavier and more absolute emanating from the worldwide cessation of all life, all movement. What chilled me was that there was no limit to this silence and there was nothing beyond it.'

Sukhbir looked up at the ceiling while two big tears coursed slowly down his cheeks.

'I am leaving this country to go and live with my father.'

* * * * * * *

CPSIA information can be obtained
at www.ICGtesting.com
Printed in the USA
LVHW040205200922
728808LV00003B/424